Drop the Act,
It's Exhausting!

Drop the Act, It's Exhausting!

FREE YOURSELF FROM YOUR SO-CALLED PUT-TOGETHER LIFE

BETH THOMAS COHEN
WITH MICHELE MATRISCIANI

TAYLOR TRADE PUBLISHING
Lanham • New York • Boulder • London

Published by Taylor Trade Publishing
An imprint of The Rowman & Littlefield Publishing Group, Inc.
4501 Forbes Boulevard, Suite 200, Lanham, Maryland 20706
www.rowman.com

Unit A, Whitacre Mews, 26-34 Stannary Street, London SE11 4AB,
United Kingdom

Distributed by NATIONAL BOOK NETWORK

British Library Cataloguing in Publication Information Available

Library of Congress Cataloging-in-Publication Data

Cohen, Beth Thomas, author.
  Drop the act, it's exhausting! : free yourself from your so-called put-
together life / Beth Thomas Cohen ; with Michele Matrisciani.
    pages cm
  ISBN 978-1-4930-0852-0 (pbk. : alk. paper) — ISBN 978-1-63076-123-3
(electronic) 1. Self-acceptance in women. 2. Self-realization in women.
3. Self-esteem in women. 4. Women—Psychology. I. Title.
  BF575.S37C64 2015
  155.3'339—dc23

2015028863

∞™ The paper used in this publication meets the minimum requirements
of American National Standard for Information Sciences—Permanence of
Paper for Printed Library Materials, ANSI/NISO Z39.48-1992.

Printed in the United States of America

To Aiden Rae & Lila James, this book is for you. . . .
I hope I make you proud!

CONTENTS

INTRODUCTION

Life Is a Circus, but That Doesn't Mean We Should Put on a Show

$\mathcal{I}$f there is an elephant in the room, I won't ignore it. I'll pitch a circus tent and step onto the podium as ringmaster of the issue. Although I've made my career in the fashion industry, I am pretty much no frills. I don't wear my husband's T-shirts or anything as bad as that, but much to my surprise, I live a pretty conventional, traditional life, which was carved out by the time I met my to-be husband in college when I was twenty. I was one of the first of my friends to get married, get pregnant, and start my own business, and part of the pleasure of all of that was sharing the ups and downs with all of them. The e-mail updates were my secret way of journaling my life's events—large and small—so I wouldn't forget them. I have short-term memory from way too much. . . .

I'm an open book, so as years went on, I e-mailed and IMed (I believe this is now a legitimate verb) less about personal details and more on musings about things that were happening to me and around me, like how the purpose of Realtors eluded me, how much I despise the stick figure family decals on the backs of minivans, the moment I first learned about mucus plugs, or the time I approached a sweaty construction worker and asked him if he expected his hoots to produce any specific desired effect. "I'm curious, sir, do you want me to whistle back?" I asked. "What are your criteria for who you holler at?" "*Do you think this will lead to drinks at the nearest pub?*" This is when people beyond my personal friends started reacting. A publicist by trade, I don't know why I was so surprised that my posts were being forwarded, and men and women of different stages and ages were applauding whatever I was saying. After all, it's what I do for a living. I am paid to get people to pay attention. But when the pregnant thirty-something receptionist at my hair salon asked me for my e-mail address after I told her there was a crap catcher in the delivery room, it was a turning point for me. Now, *I* actually believed what came out of my mouth had value.

Just like me, so many women don't realize the value of their own opinions or observations. It kills me to see so many of us go through the motions of etiquette or political correctness or just plain insecurity and shyness. We "people please," go along with the herd, or nod in agreement with an ignorant/arrogant boss and then lose ourselves in the process. In short, we act, and adopt many acts to cover up what we really believe is true. We forget who we really are and what we really want, until we become clones of each other. (I don't think there needs to be one more person in the world walking around wearing a Tory Burch flat.) Even worse, we lose the opportunity for real growth and real interpersonal connection by avoiding speaking the truth about how we feel or what we think and how we see the world through our own eyes. I call this phenomenon adopting the act.

Speaking of, here's how my eyes see my world: it's the freaking UN in my house!

I am half-black, half-white, and married to a Jewish guy. I can't do the math to figure out exactly what that makes my two little girls, because I refuse to do math. But for a Cluster F like me, the fashion world works—it's an arena in which it doesn't matter what you are; everyone is so superficial, all they are looking for is *what*, or, more appropriately, *who* you are wearing. The superficiality that surrounds me helps me avoid the need to feel I have to "label myself," but at the same time is a world that is defined by the idea that "to look good is to feel good," which has been somewhat of a double-edged sword in my career life. I always had this feeling that there was more out there for me. That I needed to do something to better the world in some way . . . and getting paid to put pretty things on pretty, privileged people for the rest of my life was not going to cut it.

I'm good at what I do, but superficial is the exact opposite of who I am and how I live. I am scarily honest. My poor husband, Brian, is the one who sees it every day. It can be such a great way to be but such a bad way, too, because people really only appreciate honesty in the abstract. Once it comes rolling toward them, the thunder scares them off. But at the end of the day, if a lab tested your blood, don't you expect the lab to call you to tell you if your results showed herpes?

Okay, clearly I wasn't the star of my high school debate team, but I hope you know what I'm saying. Everyone in my immediate life knows what I'm saying, because I am the person who "just says it." All this "stuff" swims in the room until it feels flooded, but nobody says anything. I didn't purposely make myself the Ambassador of Saying It Like It Is and certainly nobody appointed me to the position of having to blow my lifeguard whistle and announce,

"Hey folks, we're drowning in bullshit here! Women and children first!" But I can't help it.

In my defense, I don't mean to be bitchy. I *do* have a filter. There's just shit I feel compelled to say, like what a complete injustice looks like. I learned from the injustices in my own life, from a very early age, to call people out on their shit, beginning with my own father. After my parents' divorce, my mom had to struggle so hard while my father, who basically had it all, lived a quarter of a mile away. No adult at the time said how fucked up this was, so I'd be the one to stick up for her. And now, I can't stop calling people out on their stupidity and selfishness. For instance, why today I feel like I need a giant sign on my shirt saying, "These kids are mine" when I walk into my local Starbucks, is beyond me. Or "No, I'm not their nanny!" Like I said, though, I do have a filter, or else I would've already made a spectacle of myself by turning to the woman behind me in line who just asked me how much "my family paid me" because she is looking for a new nanny herself, and saying, "Why don't you remove yourself from my face until you open your eyes and notice we live in a melting pot!" And finally, I really can't keep my mouth shut when I see how some families define their relationships with their family members by measuring the amount that they do or don't do for each other! Do we have to keep count? Do we have to measure these things as a family or can we just do what we can do for each other and hope that we all contribute in some way?

I choose not to ignore the uncomfortable things because how will we ever be able to move past what bothers us? It's incredibly liberating to get it out there, discuss, and move on and hope that the conversation is productive and leads to a better understanding of how each person feels.

Honestly? A Book about Honesty?

I do want to write a book about honesty, but when I say honest, I am not talking about it in the "Thou shalt not lie" way. I'm talking about going against the grain on one of the most obnoxious and insulting pieces of propaganda out there: "Act as if." I've seen this little ditty in dozens of self-help books, and it's supposed to help us "imagine" and "visualize" ourselves "as if" we were doing or acting in the way we hope to (so then it can come true!). Here's a concept: Why not act "as." *As*. That's it. Nothing more than that—just act *as*. *As* you are. *As* I am. Wouldn't that be nice? To drop the act, let down the guard, the barrier, and the "imagining," and let women see each other's vulnerabilities, imperfections, and neuroses, and then laugh them off. Be unabatingly real, by shouting, "I know I seem like I'm 'put together,' but I'm not, and frankly, pretending isn't worth it anymore!" Oh, that would feel so good. Maybe if women can get to this place, we can all get some real connection going again, like the type we had when we were young.

You know the friend you met when you were eight or nine years old? The one with whom you made friendship bracelets, learned to French braid hair, traded stickers, and played hopscotch? Can you remember how vulnerable that age is and just how raw you were? When you were with this friend, which was probably as close to 24/7 as you could get, you were simply yourself without any outside influences; you were exactly *as* you were. I have a friend like that. I met her at camp and she was my maid of honor, and to this day, twenty-seven years after we met, we love each other. So no matter what happens between the ages of nine and ninety-nine, you can put on different clothes, have different careers, have more money, have less money, marry very different types of guys, and it will never make a difference. You just know each other's true essence.

As a grown-up, I still hold relationships to that standard. I like the genuineness of it. I feel safe in that way of being. I don't like or trust people who aren't themselves. When people are open with me, I feel comfortable, connected.

My Circus of Contradiction

I think I was compelled at an early age to divulge the most authentic side of myself to most anyone who could take it. When you go to private/prep school and have a mom who was a debutante in St. Louis, is a member of the Junior League, and married a black man from New York City's Upper East Side projects, you pretty much have a hard time concealing who you are or where you come from. Just looking at me, it's pretty obvious.

Race was a big issue in 1975, the year I was born, and I was a mixed-race child. I didn't like people assuming things about me that they didn't know, but when you wear your heritage like a neon sign, people just think they have the right to judge you or try to figure you out. So, in order to avoid all of that, I tried to beat people at their own game by just putting myself out there as a way to deflect prejudgments and assumptions; it was my so-called armor. My rationale was, if I let you see what you get from the start, you won't have to wrongly assume *anything* about me. I'll beat you at your own game. I guess, like, I was playing offense for my entire life. I'll control the ball, so you don't take it from me and run it in the wrong direction. But what's even truer is that I am more defensive when it comes to other people. It kills me to see anyone stuck in a bad or negative moment. Let's enjoy the moment, not be deterred or distracted in our heads thinking negative things that are useless and counterproductive. If you put it out there, and just say it, it's very Zen, like watching a thought in your mind and letting it go.

So, I play offense and defense, which keeps my mind very busy, to say the least. I live a life of contradiction. I require authenticity, but I work in a world that is superficial as hell. I have knowledge of things, but they don't define me. My father had money, but my mom no longer lived that life of privilege after her parents disowned her for marrying my dad (which resulted in divorce anyway). I went to a private school and traveled first class with my father to places like Hawaii, while my mother struggled every day. My friends drove luxury cars like Mercedes and Range Rovers, and I had a Honda Civic, only after I earned it. These contradictions in my life certainly were not invisible to pretty much anyone. So what did I wind up doing? I pitched the tent, and invited all of the elephants in the room to join my circus!

So, instead of being afraid to talk about my mixed race, my parents' divorce, the grandparents I never knew, I talked *more* about them. And the strangest thing happened. I realized how uncomfortable and fearful people are of the truth. To this day, I still don't know why. To me the truth doesn't hurt. It heals. When I have conversations with a person I want it to be like a breath of fresh air for both of us, and that can't happen if I'm not honest. It is music to my ears when I hear, "I never knew that," or "Nobody ever told me, until you," or "I love that you just said that." And after so many years of acting so many different ways, lying to fit in, and making myself a carbon copy of the people around me, it's refreshing to finally be okay with the person I was always meant to be.

The Point Is . . .

Aside to always keep the Ninth Commandment, the point is I hope this book inspires women to give themselves permission to talk about the things they want to talk about but don't feel like they can. How long can any one of us keep up appearances, and live in fear of alienation if we dare express our true views and justify our feelings? It doesn't always have to be so neat and pretty. Once in a while it's okay to step in some elephant dung. You know that saying, "If your friend jumped off the George Washington Bridge, would you?" In short, just because everyone else is doing it does not mean you have to, too. Isn't that the lesson we learn (especially girls) when we are introduced to peer pressure at the ripe age of twelve? Doesn't that still apply even when we are in our thirties? Do we really all have to have the same Chanel bag, Moncler coat, and Prada boots? Or can we all choose things we love for ourselves because we love them, *not* because they propel us into a certain stratosphere where we *think* we can be accepted?

If you yearn for honest, authentic, and intimate relationships and figure that you're not alone in your thinking, you are right. Imagine a world in which you can talk to another person about real issues big and small and not be judged. In which you can drop the act and not be ashamed of what is really going on in your life. From whether to stay in a relationship for the sake of the children to how much pot can you smoke and still be normal. Can you flash someone and not get arrested? And if you ever get arrested, do you one day tell your kids? Ah, the freedom that can come with broaching some of these subjects. We might just quit therapy!

I wrote this book to cross the divisive lines of shame and insecurity and scrutiny that we have been trained to cover up by acting as if we have it all "put together!" The woman who feels compelled to deck herself out to go grocery shopping, not because she is going somewhere after but because she feels like if she doesn't she will be judged by other women. Or the professional career mom who feels like she has to keep her work life separate for fear of non-working moms judging her for not showing up to school assemblies! Or the full-time mother who feels she constantly has to justify herself to the working mom! And the woman who just knows she will truly find happiness if she just lost weight. I wrote it to make you laugh, because if I say something that makes someone chuckle or even text me "LMAO," or "OMG," that is my confirmation that I just validated another person because, to me, something is funny because there is truth to it. I also wrote it because, frankly, there is shit I know that I learned the hard way, and I figured you might want to know it, too. Am I going to give you all the answers to life's greatest mysteries? No. Am I going to give you the recipe for an elixir that will poison your mother-in-law? No. Will I tell you it's okay to have that one-night stand? Maybe. (I had a one-night stand once, but I married him.)

I will, however, most definitely tell you that I have longer and stronger relationships of all types (family, love, friendship, work) because I am a straight shooter; because I have learned to drop the various acts we adopt in our culture to cover up the "flaws." If you cut out the bullshit, and just drop the act, you get where you need to get a lot faster. None of us have time or energy for the dance . . . it's exhausting.

Pièce de Résistance

Before we move on to the rest of the book, I will leave you with this. You already know I am a publicist in the fashion industry, but I haven't mentioned that I specialize in accessories—shoes, bags, jewelry, scarves, hats, broaches, and so on. I know I am not saving lives every day when I help market a new brand, but I do think accessories are a powerful tool for a wardrobe update and an emotional lift. One steamin' piece can change a look. Accessories identify and accentuate your personality with little maintenance or adjustment to your current clothing; and it never matters what size you are one month to the next.

When you decide to drop the act, speak your mind, tell the truth, listen to others without judgment, open up dialogues, and even welcome a little debate, it changes *your* entire look. Wearing your authenticity on the outside, as if it were a medallion, is a message of your true personality—an added accessory that updates your life and enhances the lives of others. I hope that all of the topics we will be discussing with fervent honesty in the following chapters—from self-esteem and aging to relationships and parenting—will inspire you to find your own way of wearing your forever piece so it will not only change your look, but complete it.

Now that's truly being put together!

1

The Act: Fake It till You Make It

Why to Drop the Act: Go off your meds, drink less wine, stop online shopping addictions, sleep more, avoid the need for disastrous coping mechanisms, and so much more!

Confidence isn't about pretending or putting on an act. Confidence springs from genuine accomplishment and work.

—Katty Kay and Claire Shipman, *The Confidence Code*

*M*y friends and I often joke that I am the one person in our circle that isn't on meds—at least not legal ones, anyway. Whether it's for sleep, anxiety, depression, or hormone replacement, my thirty- and forty-something friends are nothing but explicit about their therapists, psychiatrists, and whether they've been upped or downed in their dosages. While even I enjoy washing down a Xanax with a glass of wine, other women are miles ahead of me, comparing the colors of their anti-whatever drugs and swapping them like stickers or baseball cards. Blue, pink, or white?

"I'll give you two blues for a white. . . ."

"How about two blues and two pinks and the white's all yours."

"Deal."

One of my good friends works in an office in which it seems that the entire staff is on various brands of SSRIs that treat clinical depression. "When I forgot mine one day, all I had to do was send out a mass e-mail and ask if anyone could spare one," she laughed. "I wound up with three offers!"

Granted, this is New York City, where comparing and contrasting RXs is as normal as a bagel and cream cheese, but I tend to think the overall stigma is decreasing, which is a great thing. But I am curious as to why so many people are on meds, or think they should be. And more important, is there something wrong with *me* that nothing is wrong with me? Or is there so much wrong with me that it surpasses anything medication can treat? (The latter is more likely.)

A whopping one in four women takes antidepressants! Some resources say it's one in three. Either statistic doesn't even hold true when it comes to the people I know. It's more like one in four DOESN'T—little old me. Now, I am not saying I don't believe in medication, nor am I saying that there aren't legitimate reasons like anxiety or depression or social anxiety to take meds. I absolutely do know this shit is real! My own daughter suffers from a clinical anxiety disorder, for which she is prescribed a cocktail. But, when I went online looking for information about medication disparities, I found this: "Whites eat three-

and-a-half times as many antidepressants as blacks." Wow! This explains it. Since, I'm half-black, I am half-happier than my all-white friends! Case closed.

Not so fast.

If black people aren't as depressed as white people (actually, there is also literature that says blacks *are* much happier than whites), then why did they invent "the blues"? Why do they sing about all the bad stuff happening to them? Why would anyone who is happy ever write lyrics like "My pockets are empty, I feel so low / If somebody loves me, ain't said so" (from "Don't Look Now, but I've Got the Blues," written by Lee Hazelwood)?

Oh, yeah . . . nothing says happiness like "the blues."

But then I realized it all makes perfect sense.

Why We're All Depressed

Actually, we're not *all* depressed. If you didn't already have a good reason to hate men (like sitting in a Weight Watchers meeting clapping while the leader hands out a BRAVO sticker to the middle-aged guy who lost ten pounds his first week while your stomach growls and you gained two pounds), you do now: According to 2011 CDC figures (dumbed down for me by blogger and statistician William M. Briggs, whom I discovered on an admittedly rudimentary Google search, and who, by the way, has amazing SEO), only 6 percent of men take antidepressants. That's probably because they're not worrying about saving the world and looking good doing it!

The diatribe of self-help out there that addresses this irksome need for women to hold the world up higher than

Atlas ever could usually prescribes a few overused clichés that really piss me off:

Take Your Oxygen First

Think Positive

Just Breathe

Rather than do any of these, I'd rather stick a needle in my eye. But the most annoying of all, and in my opinion, the most detrimental to women's emotional health is the motto "Act as if." This whole idea that if you want to be successful or perceived as successful, act *as if* you are. It's the cousin of "Fake it until you make it," which is equally annoying because the faking and acting is what, in my opinion, is driving women to pop Cymbalta with chasers of Corona Light.

Nearly every glamorous, wealthy, successful career woman you might envy now started out as some kind of schlep.

—Helen Gurley Brown

After I was guilty of trying to fit in with others at the expense of who I really was, I thought back to a time in my life when I had no other choice but to act *as if* I was exactly who I was. I found that the attitude and the freedom I had back then were what I wanted to emulate in my adulthood. From grade four to grade seven, I was the most comfortable and confident about myself. I suppose at nine, I had a degree of self-awareness without the self-loathing that comes along in adolescence, and age twelve was still young enough to do kid stuff (at least back in my day) and place my priorities on buying Madonna CDs and lusting after Mark Wahlberg.

I remember vividly going to all of these Bar and Bat Mitzvahs, over-the-top parties in over-the-top venues. Clearly I was never having one of them, since (a) I was not Jewish, and (b) my mom didn't have money. I would go to these events sporting a French braid and a taffeta dress and dance my ass off with my friends. I didn't notice at the time the jeers from the adults in the room as I "got down" in a room full of strangers who wouldn't know a *Soul Train* line if Don Cornelius had started one there himself! Next to the staff, I was definitely the darkest-skin person in the catering hall. But the best part of all is that I had no idea; I would just throw down and enjoy every moment of it. Being self-conscious wasn't yet a concept. Oh, to be young and clueless again! There was no act, no pretending to be someone I wasn't. I was just me, and it felt so incredibly good to be that person.

Do you remember you when you just woke up in the morning, got dressed for school, and were just you? You might have to dig really deep to get there, but hopefully you can because this is the place I want us all to get back to, the place of purity, nonjudgment, and camaraderie—the pre–junior high stage. The part that is in touch with our true essences, where not only do we not care what people think, we aren't even aware that they have the option to form an opinion about us in the first place! I've come full circle, from the young naïve to sticking tooth-brushes down my throat to fit in with the group to not giving a tiny shit what people think. No longer do I try to be someone I am not—some of that came with age, some of it with kids, some of it with not having the time or energy anymore because pretense requires effort.

Acting "as if" means you have to be "on" all the time, and I just want to sleep. So now, I say what I mean and I mean what I say, and I feel a lot healthier living this way. It's not always easy, because when you say shit that people are thinking but would never say, it can leave a bad taste in their mouth, but it sure feels good on my end—and a hell of a lot more liberating!

Because of all of this and a whole lot more, I am of the opinion that it's not clinical depression that millions of women are treating with these antidepressants or anything we do to deal; it's the fact that in an attempt to *act as if they have it all*, women are overworked, underpaid, undersexed, undernourished, and overstressed. Have the career, your own bank account and retirement plan; live your life juicing for dinner and Spinning sixteen times

---

There, I Said It! Underneath the Many Layers of Lululemon, You Might Just Find a Lassie!

It's a brand some of you may or may not know, and if you don't, all you have to do is google images of "suburbia" followed by the word "Lululemon," and you will find a plethora of deplorable photographs of women doing everything in their posh exercise wear but exercising! This is a minor part, but still a part of this "act as if" bullshit. We hide behind our brands and the perception that we are just picking up a few organic items before we head off to our hot yoga class. Oh, please. A lot of my best girlfriends do sport the brand—even I do on occasion—however, it's hard to differentiate us from the ones who wear it and use it as their armor! Hiding behind brands is one of the quickest and easiest (albeit, not so cheap) ways to adopt the act. Douse me in designer duds and then I will feel more secure, more "like" everyone else.

---

a week; show up for your kid's stupid school Halloween parade; remember to send in a can of pumpkin pie mix for the pointless mock Thanksgiving at your other kid's school; and get the bikini waxed for the "date night" that your husband will no doubt fall asleep in the middle of. And this is a good week! So we turn to our happy pills and our wine (more on that in chapter 4) and our online shopping addictions, and we numb, we cope, we self-soothe, only to continue on with this psychotic way of life, weighed down by expectations we place on ourselves, our spouses, and our children—setting us up for failure and burnout. Of course, we think we need a doctor to save us, and believe you me I am not an exception! But we don't always, which at first was only my uninformed opinion, until I found this intriguing figure that actually backs me up. Go me.

A study published in April 2013 in the journal *Psychotherapy and Psychosomatics* found that nearly two-thirds of a sample of more than five thousand patients who had been given a diagnosis of depression within the previous twelve months did *not* meet the criteria for major depression.

What's this indicate? That there are a whole hell of a lot of us, looking for a coping mechanism for the pressures of living in an extremely unstable and volatile economic, political, and social environment, and seeking it in the form of a happy pill. The interesting thing is it doesn't seem to be working. In fact, it's like depression is a contagious disease, traveling through the air and infecting more and more of us, making us fearful of this natural emotion. Why fear it? Which brings me back to the blues, and my epiphany. What if we dropped the "act as if" act. What if we stopped putting pressure on ourselves to outwardly appear as if we are tremendously happy, fulfilled, successful, functional, put together, and have it all? What if we sang the blues instead?

The reason why the blues was invented was to provide a creative, productive way to *vent* and communicate on a large scale. To share with a community the truth about what it is like to be them to a community that gets it.

I don't have enough money
I'm lonely
My woman/man's gone
I'm oppressed
I'm scared
I'm in a rut

Similarly, women could be a part of a phenomenal, like-minded, supportive community if we just stop faking it in an attempt to "make it" and instead sing loud and proud:

I didn't get enough sleep
I'm tired to the core
And if you come near me
I'll walk out that door
'Cause I'm a woman. . . .

Imagine your audience of downtrodden, fed-up women, hootin' and hollerin' back at you, à la a Chicago jazz and blues club, "You go!" "Sing it, sister," "Amen!" You'd feel great. Hell, just thinking about coming out with all my shit and having it received by cheers makes me want to run out and patent a whole new type of karaoke machine.

You have a willing and waiting audience desperate to hear your faux pas, your gripes, your grievances, your grunt work, your inequity, and your fatigue over "faking it until you make it." Make what? Make yourself crazy?

You'll all be a lot saner, if you drop the act, let it all hang out on the dance floor, and start being truthful about what it's like to be you. That way, you will get to know her better, too, and like very much what you see underneath the guise.

2

The Act: Love and Marriage—I Have It Made

Why to Drop the Act: Because sometimes all you feel like is the maid—and so does everybody else

We are afraid to care too much, for fear that the other person does not care at all.

—Eleanor Roosevelt

*I*magine your life were a Kansas farmhouse, in which you've been holed up for a good part of the month. On most days, the house sways beneath gusts of unrelenting demands to feed, clothe, and bathe as well as mounting bills and childish bickering between your spouse and you over something as minor as a dirty coffeepot. Somehow the house manages to never quite fall in on itself, but it comes close enough for you to go in search of respite. You spend countless minutes inside your head, mentally escaping to your bedroom, where you slam the door behind you, draw the blinds, and sing sweetly to yourself a song filled with idealistic wishes and desire—probably not in the company of the dog, because right now you hate him, too.

The few minutes alone help you feel impervious enough to venture a peek out the window. Now, you are a spectator of the very tornado that activated your flight response. Resentment and cynicism ride past you on a bicycle—the wind is ripping you a new asshole, *you wanted this, you asked for this, now look.*

The howling and screaming outside threaten to blow through the glass, so you fall onto the bed and with all your might smother your screams with a pillow, getting a little high on your own carbon dioxide. *Cool.*

You must've fallen asleep because when you wake, you feel the drama and the guilt and the exhaustion in free fall; your farmhouse is descending in a slow-motion spin—the outside elements no longer stalwart enough to carry the burden. What goes up must come down, and the mania you let sweep you away drops you hard on your ass with a thud. You wince. You sit on the bed, temples pulsating, disoriented; you can't remember what exactly it was that brought you to this stealth emotional hideaway in the first place. The storm has subsided now, yet the relief you wanted hasn't come. Instead it's more ominous than when you initially took cover. *Did I really say those things to him? Oh boy, I'm in for it.* You know there is nothing normal about this kind of quiet—the kind that scientists might study—so thick that the soundlessness produces a ringing in your ears, as if you are being reprimanded by an otherworldly dimension. Nothing good can come out of the blankness that surrounds you, because where there is such silence, there is no . . . life.

You damn the quiet, and with a visceral desperateness you run to the very door you locked yourself behind, and with both hands on the knob, pray it isn't jammed for good, *please let all the craziness still be out there.* You are not sure to whom you are talking, but you continue, *I'm sorry I lost it, please don't have let my selfish thoughts come true. I didn't mean a word.* You open the door, your body hiding behind it, pretending it were a wooden shield. And behold! Life. Plusher than ever. In fact, in Technicolor. Noise, beautiful noise. Mess. Dirty coffeepot. Muttering husband. You sashay past the door, basking in the thanklessness of this peculiar place. You twirl within the humdrum reality of this life, *your life*, delicately gliding your fingertips over dish towels as if they were a rare species of orchid, and you realize the miracles that have surrounded you *all along* in your mundane Kansas farmhouse.

And that, my dear friends, is a long-term relationship.

Thirteen years after marrying my husband, Brian, I have diagnosed myself a little schizophrenic, sort of like the story above. How else could I explain my ability to love and hate, cry tears of joy and anguish, and feel resentment and guilt for feeling resentful—all in the same minute? But as Sam Smith sings, "I know I'm not the only one." How many times have we heard stories of parents who found their kids after losing them at the beach, proclaiming, "When I find this kid, I am going to beat the shit out of him"? Or, the woman who is disappointed year after year by her husband's choice in her birthday gifts (or lack thereof) but goes on to defend his thoughtfulness to her nosy, opinionated mother. Yup, metaphorically speaking, being in a long-term relationship is like living in the eye of an emotional twister—enough to send any woman to her bedroom for a Dorothy Gale–inspired time-out.

I could trace the origin of my own twister back to the day I gave birth to our first child, Aiden. While the myth is that there is no pleasant moment during labor, and that women prefer to capitalize on the moment by cursing out their significant others, there is a moment when you look at your partner and think, *Wow, I love you. I mean, really, I love you, I didn't know how much until now. I cannot believe what we are doing together. This is huge.*

After the baby is born, you operate in a dream state, enabled by baby nurses (or in my case, my mother) and lactation nurses and every other kind of nurse doing *everything* for you, all so you can bond with your baby and stare at her in awe. You find it hopelessly romantic that your hubby (whom you are now calling "hubby") is compelled to squeeze himself next to you on your twin-size hospital bed, hold you while you hold your baby, and smell the top of your newborn's head. *This is exactly how I imagined it.*

Then . . . the sky darkens a bit, the wind picks up. Your doctor signs the discharge forms, which is when reality hits. *I'm taking this kid with me? Like, in that car seat that I lamented over at Buy Buy Baby?* The first step out of this hospital will mark the next eighteen years (at least) of your life, so what do you do? You and hubby make like Bonnie and Clyde and sinisterly steal every article of baby supply out of the drawers—wipes, diapers, pacifiers, and as many blue-and-green-striped rags that you *think* you'll swaddle your kid in. (Note: later I found out, these items were ours for the taking anyway.) In your last moment of ever being coddled, an attendee pushes you out in a wheelchair and then as if you were in a wheelbarrow, dumps you into the

hospital corridor: "Don't let the sliding glass doors nip you in the ass on the way out."
Did you just hear that?
It's twister time.

Home. Ah, real life, family life, and the thoughts that float in your head in response. *How can someone I love so much bring me so much pain?* And you're not talking about your child! How can you have loved your spouse so much forty-eight hours ago and in the blink of an eye fantasize about throwing him in front of a tractor trailer? How could the day he said, "Make room for Daddy" on the hospital bed lead you to design a custom-made super king–size bed so you can sleep with the state of Maine in between you?

At first I likened my "hospital love" for Brian as a response to being so close to danger. After all, there is something to be said about long fluorescent-lighted hallways, gurneys, IVs, and being surrounded by life-saving beeping machines, heart monitors, and scrubs. It's very *Grey's Anatomy*, and I was being coached and loved by my very own McDreamy.

But at home, there's no threat of dying, or even the ability to pretend you are. Now, it's you, him, and the kid. The only machine you might remotely hear is suctioned to your tits, and it sounds like ducks dying a slow death in perfect cadence to "See Saw, Knock on the Door." For me, at home, there were a few exchanges of loving looks and quick kisses, but for the most part, I just wanted to smack Brian in the face for doing this to me, as I am sure he wanted to smack me. Postbaby love does not conquer all; it simply prevents us from throwing the other person out . . . forever!

The good thing is, our mutual disdain for each other in those early baby days made me curious, so I did some research on the topic. I was worried that I was somehow not on the right path, at least not the path that I have assumed most women are on once they are married with a baby—all their dreams have come to fruition, they *have it made*. I simply googled "I just had a baby and hate my husband." Holy shit. You can google any word combo these days and get a crapload of answers. The first page of results not only showed me articles on the exact topic, but were from some credible sources. From Huffington Post and Baby Center to About.com and WhattoExpect.com to The Bump and even *Daily Mail* in the UK—women across the world were hating their husbands after baby! What a relief! I was now a proud member of a Twisted Sisterhood.

What I discovered was that good old Mother Nature was actually hard at work, which is a really nice way of saying Goddamn Hormones. It wasn't *really* me who was repulsed by the thought of being near my husband; it was nature's way of guaranteeing all of my attention went to the baby, ensuring her survival. But more important, ensuring there wasn't a chance IN HELL that we'd be making another one anytime soon!

So before you go thinking there is something wrong with you or that something is possibly broken in your relationship, blame it on biology. "Honey, I hate you because I'm *supposed* to." Just as chemistry played a part in bringing you two together, chemistry shall keepeth you apart.

Idealism Is for Idiots!

While my fickle feelings toward my husband were more pronounced after baby, this chapter is focused more on the mystery of being in love and in a committed relationship, kids or no kids. Charles Bukowski said, "Love is what is burned away from the horizon of reality." Sounds cynical, but it's really not. If enough of us would heed this as more of a warning about going into love with certain expectations than a warning about getting involved in the first place, there might be fewer divorces. Or at the very least, fewer emotional twisters that send us running for our bedrooms!

Expectations, we all have them. But when it comes to our partners—especially in the early stages of commitment—expectations are, unfairly, as high as the moon. I don't know what it is about deciding to take the relationship to the next level that turns us into fools of idealism—they don't call it "playing house" for nothing. But look, it's not our faults. There's been plenty of research that explains the seven-year itch, the various states of relationships, etc. The early love stage has been compared to being drugged, literally. I read once that when we fall in love the only difference between being high on drugs and high on love is that being an addict of love is legal. And, c'mon, everyone knows that when we're high or drunk, we tend to say things . . . make promises . . . feel positively about people or things that are otherwise pretty mundane. *Look at all the beautiful colors, dude.* Knowing this makes all the difference if you are going to make it in your committed relationship when you're comin' down.

Brian and I met during a sex-charged encounter in college at an age at which you can sleep with just about anyone, at any time, and still get up and pat yourself on the back the next day. The guilt does not set in right away, if at all, and you are in the prime of your youth in terms of how fucking awesome you look. Needless to say, we were both feeling and screwing on point! My reminiscing is bringing a tear to my eye.

Women can fake an orgasm, but men can fake an entire relationship.

—Sharon Stone

Twenty years later, the coming down phase has lasted a bit longer than the initial drugged year and we can't help but look at each other in a very different light—a UV light, the absolute worst kind of light. The light, like the years, enhances all of the imperfections and flaws, but here we are still both chugging along like the Little Engine That Could. Our relationship has turned up so many different avenues that sometimes it's hard to know which one we are currently on; some days it's easy street, others, the long haul stuck in bumper-to-bumper traffic on the New Jersey Turnpike. *Get me the fuck off this goddamn road. Road rage!*

I don't think there would be all of those insanely funny jokes about marriage if they weren't true! At some point or another we want to kill each other, but at the same time we always are able to move past that emotion, and back to the one when we remember why it is that we are together. Which brings us back to the emotional twister.

What do you do to keep the wind at bay? How do you pin down one of the happy personalities of your inner Sybil? And how do you remind yourself that the twister is just a passing storm, and not a devastating tsunami to your relationship? Any relationship needs to have its ups and downs or you can't realistically build a life together. That's growth; like a muscle, you tear it down to build it up. If I were still holding on to idealistic love, wishing for the days when Brian and I were carefree and running barefoot in the park and all of that crazy nonsense, I wouldn't deserve to be in this marriage.

"Words without actions are the assassins of idealism." Herbert Hoover said that, about what, I don't know, but it says a lot to me about when idealism goes out the window. When the things we said when we were high on love (a.k.a., under the influence of the hormone oxytocin—ironically, the same hormone that is produced that makes your partner repulsive so you can fall in love with your baby)—wind up being just words backed up with absolutely no action. Or, worse, when the drug incites an action only for that action to never be repeated again, once the effect of the drug wears off. Case in point, my friend Melissa, who experienced one of those love-at-first-sight storybook romances and was married ten months to the day of her first encounter with Marcus. Unbeknownst to her, Marcus put a lot of thought into their first Christmas together and showered his new wife with the most thoughtful gifts that made Melissa's sister so jealous she couldn't bear to watch Melissa opening them (her older sister had been married five years by then). First up was an electronic picture frame with their wedding song playing to a chronological pictorial of their courtship, wedding, and honeymoon. Next, three handpicked outfits that he imagined she would "make look terrific," followed by a gift certificate for a massage because she "works so damn hard." Overwhelmed with pride for reeling in the catch of a lifetime, Melissa wiped tears away and went to kiss Marcus passionately. But not so fast! There was still the stocking gift. The pièce de résistance, a diamond-and-sapphire tennis bracelet. Poor shmuck meant well, but boy did he not realize he would never be able to keep up with himself. Idiot raised his own bar *way* the hell high.

Fast-forward seven years and two children later, Melissa opened her one gift beneath the tree on Christmas morning and marveled at her husband's effort: a keychain Breathalyzer! If idealism hadn't already been killed years before, this would've been the perfect assassin.

The Real Couple Killer

They say money issues are the number one reason people break up, and yes, the stress could be enough to kill an army; however, I think it's boredom bordering on apathy that does everyone in. Actually, I'll take that one step further; it's boredom and apathy that are swept under the rug while everyone puts on their little happy faces, acting the part: "I have it made."

For reasons that I think are pretty obvious, I've never been a fan of Barbie, but walk around town and watch these PTA moms act like they are the next coming of Barbie and Ken, when they really feel more like Skipper, the awkward little sister, married to Ken's douchebag cousin. I say drop the act!

Beware of monotony; it's the mother of all the deadly sins.

—Edith Wharton

What's so wrong with being bored? If you don't let it blow things out of proportion, nothing. It's natural. I mean, how long can you love the same cubicle, the same kitchen, the same dinner food? Why can't we just accept that at one point or another in any aspect of life, we lose interest for a while, without turning it into a life crisis that renders us to delusionally seek out some "better" alternative? Instead, people try to pretend they're not bored only to secretly look for entertainment by friending old high school boyfriends on Facebook or engaging in some lame pickup conversation at a bar just because it feels titillating. We need attention, which is normal. It's not a bad thing. Too many people are ashamed of this fact. I think at some point men and women in long-term relationships begin to feel invisible, ignored, or taken for granted, so put your heads together and address the reality of the situation: Adulthood is fucking Groundhog Day! Misery loves company, so if you're miserable, I say, invite your partner IN! The more the merrier to this pity party.

The only real security is not in owning or possessing, not in demanding or expecting, not in hoping, even. Security in a relationship lies neither in looking back to what it was, nor forward to what it might be, but living in the present and accepting it as it is now.

—Anne Morrow Lindbergh

And in all fairness to bored couples across the globe, we don't really have a lot of good advice to pick from when it comes to finding ways of improving our relationships, which is probably why the *Fifty Shades of Grey* phenomenon happened. Housewives are bored enough to embrace S&M!

We're told if we want to find the "magic" again, we should plan more date nights. But given the fact that more women last year considered asking their husband to start swinging, I'd say that dates are not even remotely what we need. On a date you still have to end it back home, where most likely your kids will be sleeping and your babysitter will need a ride. Ah, yeah . . . no thank you!

Next up is advice by sexless couples who actually landed book deals by writing about how they "forced" themselves to have sex every day, no matter what, calling it an experiment. (God, and I thought it was ludicrous that *I* got a book deal!) I mean, really? Doing it under duress? This is what we've come to? Unless you are getting paid to have sex with the same person every day, I cannot understand why anyone would do this to themselves for free.

Look, I get how these couples arrived at this desperate place, but is this our best hope for advice? Again, it's no wonder most women prefer to act like everything is great—it takes less effort! For these couples turned authors, sex was the thing they wanted to do to reconnect, but I say it's also the thing we do to bribe each other to get other things done. As in, "If you sit through this awards dinner with me, I'll blow you tonight. If you don't, I will withhold sex for as long as I possibly can, and that can be *really* long."

Sex is a must with your partner. How much and what you do with him is up to you, but if you have to force yourselves, then you need to figure out what's beneath that. Maybe it's boredom, or maybe you're just freaking tired all the time, maybe you sincerely hate each other, to which, I say, you should consider picking up a different book. At times I wish I could put a bag over Brian's head and paste a photo of Mark Wahlberg on it, and I am sure he visualizes a ton of shit to put over my head, too. The important thing is that once you open your eyes and see the person you committed to, you're not actually disappointed. *Oh, gee whiz, I thought I was riding Marky Mark this whole time. Good vibrations.*

Advice I can get behind would include dropping all the pretense in relationships, and stopping being so apathetic about what's happening behind closed doors. That means communication, but the honest kind, not the have-him-guess-how-I-really-feel conversation. Do you really prefer to seethe than to be honest? You'll always hate your date nights because you planned them, so why have them? Just tell him. Or the fact that it bothers you that his life hasn't changed one bit since you've had kids, and you hate him for it, or that when he says he'll "babysit" the kids, it makes you feel like they're your sole responsibility.

My grandmother always told me, "Find someone who loves you just a little bit more than you love them." She had a point, and she would know . . . she could often be seen throwing jewelry out of her car sunroof in a rage a good twenty years into her marriage. Clearly the marriage ended in divorce, but her advice did sound good in one way, that you love each other hard and fight hard with each other. It's a true test when you add kids to the mix, and you can't possibly keep up the act when they do come, because all you want to do is murder each other and blame the other for all the stress and misery. You need to be able to sustain the divorce threats and booze-filled rants (one of you at a time), to wake up in the morning and realize why you are there. Marriage is tough, impossible really, so as long as you can both drop the act and let your "true colors come shining through" (thanks, Cindy Lauper), you will be all right.

Just Laugh . . . a Lot!

Laugh a lot: Instead of forcing themselves to have sex every day, couples would get along better if they forced themselves to laugh together every day. Same hormones,

There, I Said It! Tell Him
Off before You Get Him Off

I am never without something to say (or so people tell me)—not sure how I should take that, but considering I am the one writing the book, I honestly don't care. I mean it took forever for me to get Brian to communicate in a way I found acceptable, and for a person who communicates for a living, that was kind of weird. Now we communicate better than we ever did before, but we also argue more than we ever did before. I think when you are a couple for so long you challenge each other in a good way when you do actually have a chance to converse. Sometimes we don't need to talk at all, and that's something that has evolved nicely in the last twenty years.

Things Women Think about but
Don't Tell Their Men . . . Unless You Are Me

1. I love you more when you help do things.
2. You're not likely to get any if I don't want to give any.
3. I am going out with my girlfriends and plan to get piss drunk, flirt with anyone and everyone (even skirts), and will love every single moment of it and not feel the least bit guilty.
4. You're way cuter when you are holding the kids.
5. Still crazy after all these years!
6. Sometimes I watch you sleep and want to suffocate you with a pillow, but then you look so peaceful for a second.
7. Don't patronize me by telling me I'm "just PMSing" or "overwhelmed," and don't dare ever tell me to "calm down," because that will guarantee I don't.
8. Just get me a goddamn card! What is so hard about this?
9. Mother's Day is much more important than my birthday.
10. I have a lot more than ten things to say, but I have a word count limit for this book.

less pressure! And the more you laugh, the more likely you will soften to each other and sex will just happen. I am always one for comedy. It's the only thing that can really get us out of an argument. Humor is the best tool in a marriage.

I was at a party recently when one of the drunk women seated at our table was confiding in me that it's been six months since she had sex (really boring sex) with her husband. She opened up a can of worms at the table, man, validating almost every woman's inactivity. It was weird and cool at the same time. Nobody was thinking they were weird because this beautiful woman in her early forties was just putting it out there, no apologies, no act. See, it's not just you!

3

The Act: I Am a Prenatal Gestating Supermom (and Have Only Gained a Pound So Far. . . .)

Why to Drop the Act: Because a realistic pregnancy means realistic parenting

You do get the pregnant mush-brain . . . you know what it's like? It's like getting stoned.

—Kate Hudson

$\mathcal{B}$efore I got pregnant, I could give two shits about classical music, but the minute the ultrasound technician matter-of-factly inched toward me with an extraterrestrial-looking dildo with a camera on its tip, John Williams's orchestral theme song for *Close Encounters of the Third Kind* sounded off in my head. *Oh great, I'm about to be vaginally probed, and all I can envision is Richard Dreyfuss. Can't I queue the theme to* Magic Mike *or something? Already, they're taking away my fun!* It was kind of apropos, since something quite alien was growing inside me, and I thought about my own close encounter, most likely under the influence, and how it's what got me in these stirrups in the first place.

I don't say this to be mean, or to imply I am not ecstatic about being a mother (oh, I hope that wasn't a spoiler; I wound up having the baby), because I am ecstatic, and it's certainly what my husband Brian and I planned and wanted. But I wasn't expecting it to dawn on me quite so quickly that pregnancy would change me in more ways than I could ever imagine. I was prepared for the physical changes (sort of), but not for the acting-out-of-character part, e.g., being responsible and mature.

My transformation began the minute I found out I was pregnant. Proudly, I admit that I was hammered that night. I had spent a long evening drinking with my husband, Brian, along with my two best childhood guy friends, Jason and Matty, followed by a little "puff puff give." Needless to say Brian and I stumbled into our apartment at around 3:30 a.m. and passed out shortly thereafter. You know when you wake up and the sun is coming up and you're still piss drunk? Well, that was me when I decided that I was bored and should pee on a stick to see if I was pregnant. We had just started trying, so I think I was just looking for shits and giggles or attempting to be ironic, as drunk people tend to. *My aim is surprisingly good,* was all I could think, until, *Hmm, it says positive.* But c'mon, even I couldn't trust a drunk person, especially when she's me. I tried to remember the line about false positives: *"There's no such thing as positives, if they're false"? No, that's not it. "False negatives happen"? No. Shit, I know. There's no such thing as . . . There's no place like . . .* I grabbed the spare pee stick and went to town on it, finally remembering the goddamn saying: "There's no such thing as false positives, only false negatives." (Which I am not sure is even true, but I felt better that I got it straight.) And whaddya know, still positive.

There I sat in the bathroom—me, myself, and my pee stick. It was still quiet in New York City, just the lone sound of taxicabs rhythmically tapping loose manhole covers in the street outside, and I felt a little foolish. While I had made the conscious decision with my husband to try for a baby, here I was . . . stunned that it had actually happened. And then it hit me. Brian wouldn't be a parent for nine more months, meaning he'd have time to warm up to the idea, go through whatever stages of emotions (or lack thereof) he would need to in order to prepare. But from the minute the double lines on that stick slowly manifested like a Polaroid picture, I had become an instant parent—just add water. No longer would I freely open a can of tuna fish without questioning whether I was treating my body like a BP oil spill. There was no time period allotted for me to get geared up, run a warm-up lap, or mourn the loss of the "old" mercury-eating, wine-guzzling, "I'll sleep when I'm dead" me. I felt like I should get scared, I mean, was I really ready to say good-bye to sushi, wine, and the mother of all necessities—coffee?! But instead of panic, a wave of knowingness rolled over me, and I felt confident and powerful. I looked the same, I peed the same, I was inebriated the same, but my body had already begun performing some mind-blowing magic trick *without me even knowing it*, or having the ability to micromanage it. In that way, I felt small and insignificant, but also big and vital. And then . . . *For fuck's sake, enough of this touchy-feely stuff. Nobody knows but me! I could go downstairs, take a shot, smoke one last cig, and it would be between God and me. Hell, I'll even have a tuna melt.* Before I could get off the toilet, though, BAM, it happened. Fun-loving, crazy, irresponsible, selfish Beth turned a corner. Instead of heading downstairs for a rendezvous with my vices, I chose to wake up Brian and share with him the good news. Let the transformation begin.

Transformation #1: Suddenly, You Can't Think without a Pregnancy To-Do List.

I truly don't understand it. The only "to-do" I thought was necessary was the one that I already did to become pregnant. But no, now we need more tasks to fill the next nine months of gestation, which I think should keep us busy enough. Don't women already do it all? Apparently not. Books, websites, magazines, reality television fill their content with propaganda of countdowns and prepping, checklists, baby-proofing, labor and delivery methods. Can't we just *be*? Can't we just have pregnancies that are quiet and contemplative like my moment in the bathroom with my pee stick? I suppose if you do want such tranquil moments, you can always add them to your to-do list—dinner with the Smiths, pick up dry cleaning, research Zen practitioners and prenatal yoga classes—but that seems to defeat the purpose. And, by the way, forget all of this if you already have a kid and this is your second pregnancy. Life is just a shit storm at that point. Ain't no to-do list that's going to help you manage any of it.

Don't misunderstand my harshness here. I am guilty as charged. I have always considered myself a pragmatic, "don't drink the Kool-Aid" kind of girl; however, once I told Brian we were going to be parents, I took on the role of "marketer's dream." I was all in and then some. If you weren't trying to sell me something, have me knock off a checklist or two, or tell me to avoid coming into contact with shrimp and cat litter (hopefully not together), I was insulted. But what I wished someone would've told me is that all of this prenatal prospecting was really an indoctrination into the act—the act of being and doing all things perfectly, "above reproach," as Emily Dickinson might've said. It's like advertising to little kids the wonderfulness of Cap'n Crunch, with the only intention of getting them hooked on sugar and branding cues. The same holds true here. Hook women into judging themselves against something other than themselves and they'll be on the marketing teat for life. And it all begins with the Pregnancy Checklist.

Generally speaking, women love quizzes and checklists. Magazines especially know this, which is why you won't see one women's magazine next month that doesn't recycle a quiz or self-assessment of some sort. When it comes to pregnancy-related checklists, it's like we are in some sort of whacked competition with ourselves to see if we can do more than we usually do (and better) while gestating a baby. Are pregnant women instinctively aware that doing something miraculous like *growing a person* will ultimately be upstaged by the act of actually having to keep that human being alive after it comes? Okay, one superhuman feat at a time. Let's not rush the drama, but we do. Our impulsive society has made our vaginas impulsive, giving new meaning to the word "snatch." As soon as we catch that sperm, we pee on a stick, upload it to the BabyCenter app on our smartphone and find out the due date. (And if you've done that, you've probably already used the ovulation app, so your smartphone could tell you when you and your partner should screw. God, that's *so* hot.) Then we plug the due date into an algorithm, and we begin a literal countdown to baby —all before any self-respecting obstetrician will agree to examine us.

What about the example set by Stone Age hunter-gatherer women in Scandinavia, who worked the fields to feed their extended families, not knowing what day it was, or how preggo they actually were? They ventured alone deeper into the field to privately squat, grunt, scream, and hoist the cord up to behold the next generation, only to get back to the *really hard* work of gathering.

When did women, the daughters of the "hear me roar" mothers, become such wusses about doing what comes naturally? When were our ferocious roars replaced with nasally whines about when to schedule a C-section? I'll tell you when, when some sadistic person added it to the Pregnancy Checklist!

According to TheBump.com, these are some of the things you should make sure you do when you are pregnant.

Weeks 1–8

- Take pregnancy test—*Would I be browsing The Bump if I didn't already do this?*
- Tell your partner the good news—*Frankly, how the hell do you know I have a partner or that it's good news? Can you say presumptuous?*
- Find an OB/GYN—*What do they mean? I'm going to need a doctor now?*
- Schedule prenatal checkup—*Isn't this a bit superfluous to the previous item? See, they just want to add tasks for the sake of adding tasks!*
- Research insurance—how does it deal with pregnancy and children?—*I don't even know how I am going to deal with pregnancy and children. . . .*

- Make sure partner has short- and long-term disability—*Is this in the event of mood swings and I disable him?*
- Figure out how pregnancy, baby, and maternity leave will affect finances—*Short answer: It will!*
- Create a savings plan for your child's future expenses—*Cart way before the horse. Let's get the kid a Pack 'n Play first.*
- Make a budget to start saving now—*Another redundant task.*

Phew! I don't know about you, but I am so relieved I had this handy dandy checklist. And I dutifully checked off each box—twice for the repeated ones. Hey, it makes me seem productive. *What a great mom I will be.*

I'm warning you that some of these checklists have sub-checklists. For instance, somewhere in the third trimester, a checklist item is "Interview pediatricians." But then, you have a checklist of questions to ask these pediatricians. One of my personal favorite checklists is a sub-checklist of the item "Pack your hospital bag." Yes, there is a checklist of things you will need to put in a suitcase.

Excuse me. I am pregnant, which sort of implies I've slept outside of my house once or twice before. Why, all of a sudden, do I need a list to tell me to pack a toothbrush, my fat underwear, slippers, and—wait for it . . . wait for it—pajamas!

Here's what's *not* on the checklist, because these pricks get off on omitting what we really need, like:

- Six months' supply of Depends for when your crotch is hemorrhaging and you have what is essentially a sixty-day-long period. Yeah, nobody mentioned *that* to you, right?

- A Do Not Disturb sign because if you opt for breastfeeding they *will* disturb you. *What is with them waking me up so much?* And if you decide not to breastfeed they will still wake you up, to tell you that you *should* breastfeed.

- A Do Not Disturb sign because if you're not breast-feeding and you've instructed nurses to feed the kid in the nursery (smart move), the disgruntled night staff will come in and freaking wake you up anyway to take your vitals way more than is vitally necessary (see above). And by the second time they wake you, your blood pressure will probably read

---

There, I Said It! Checklist or Litmus Test?

I had been checking off boxes for nine months, so when it came to questionnaires, I became a bit trigger happy. After I had Lila, my second daughter, a "specialist" came in to speak to me about recreational drug and alcohol use. While I was in labor (and being admitted to the hospital), I was asked to read through another questionnaire, because what woman who can barely stand or speak wouldn't want to read through a document and answer question after question coherently? But I digress. Next to a blank box was the question: "Have you ever used recreational drugs?" *Easy one. Check.* Con-traction. After I cursed *Lamaze for Dummies* and got a hold of myself, the next empty box stared at me. "Do you drink al-cohol?" *Poor fools don't know me at all. Check.* Contraction.

So when the counselor came in to "have a talk with me," my straight-as-an-arrow mother just looked at me as if she wanted to disown me. Apparently, the questionnaire had asked if I drank alcohol and did drugs *during* my pregnancy.

---

higher than the last read. *Let me sleep through the night one last time!*

Transformation #2: You Become a Feral Animal, a Voracious Eater.

This ain't no hunger pang. It's more like a cramp, and it makes you mean as hell. You are insatiable . . . so hungry you will stop a meeting, stop traffic, stop the presses, to get what you want—FOOD! You'll be quite unapologetic about it, too, especially when you show no mercy toward the cook who doesn't prepare your food just the way you envisioned! I said *Rice-a-Roni, not rigatoni, YOU MORON!*

Transformation #3: If You're Like Me during My First Pregnancy, You Might Feel Like Absolute Crap, Most of the Time.

I was pregnant way before the Duchess of Cambridge made morning sickness chic. For me just a piece of fruit or toast with jam would catapult me into an undignified tailspin of nausea, vomiting, fatigue, irritability, and water retention. What they don't tell you is that pregnant puking is not like party puking. When you're drunk, there's a sense of relief—the poison has been discharged, and in less than thirty minutes, you dive into the cold pizza that's sat out all night and quite possibly pour another drink. *Hair of the dog.* During pregnancy, however, you lose your lunch as well as the ability to imagine yourself ever eating again. Breathing makes you puke; there is just no relief. I really hope this isn't you, but if it is, get ready to experience the next transformation.

Transformation #4: You Begin to Give Credence to Old Wives' Tales.

If you're sick all the time or uglier than you usually are (and people will let you know), you're having a girl. "Girls suck the pretty right out of you." If your bump is smaller, of course, you're having a boy. In your former nonpregnant life, you'd fantasize about lining up such idiots and shooting them, but today, *well, maybe there's something to it.* . . . Get a hold of yourself!

Transformation #5: You Are Horny as Hell.

Some of my friends never watched a porn video in their life or played with a sex toy until their second trimesters (how unfortunate for them). The increase in sex drive has got to have something to do with your subconscious telling you to do all the dirty deeds now, so you can remember them with fondness later when you cease to have sex and loathe your partner more than you ever have before!

The likelihood that you'll be passing mirrors naked and loving what you're seeing might decrease (hell, who am I kidding, it will cease to exist), so it's nice that your partner desires you when you're pregnant. Get it out of both your systems now, because when it comes to sex after baby, you most likely won't want your partner to even look at you for a good six months or quite possibly a full year!

Transformation #6: You Begin Acting Out of Character.

You are kinder to strangers, and they are kinder to you. You'll spend a lot more time taking care of yourself when you are pregnant, as does your mate. Sometimes it's good

There, I Said It! The Boy Mom Club

The perfect pregnant people who perpetuate the act say things like "Oh, I don't care what I'm having, as long as it's healthy." Bullshit. There is a secret society of women that I am outing right now, and this society is composed of boy moms. My unscientific poll has revealed that nine out of ten moms cried when their sonogram tech told them their first child would be a boy. One of my friends cried for a weekend; another talked with her therapist about it for at least three sessions. While this might sound like a terrible thing for a woman to do, I say, what's the big deal about admitting you were upset? Of course you're upset. You've spent your entire life caring for a vagina, and now you're expected to understand penis maintenance (which I hear is so much easier). And until adolescence, you hated boys. They were stupid and pointless, and now that you're in a relationship with one, you realize they're still kind of stupid and pointless! Now you are actually contributing to adding one more male to the world? Isn't that being an accessory to a crime? Who will inherit your Cabbage Patch Dolls; who will be swaddled in the pink blanket your grandmother crocheted before she died? What about your jewelry?

Don't beat yourself up for feeling in this way. Every boy mom goes through it! And then, my unscientific follow-up research revealed that every boy mom out there would never ever trade in for a girl. I had a friend tell me that she decided that being "chosen" as a boy mom was the biggest responsibility in the world, and one she was honored to be given. After all, it takes amazing women to raise amazing men! And you're an amazing woman!

and sometimes it's bad, but you'll notice you are more emotional than ever. During her last trimester, my very pulled-together friend Lauren was in the passenger seat driving home from her sister's dinner party, when her husband swerved around what they later discovered was a lame mama cat and her lame kittens. Lauren couldn't stop crying. She ran to the litter of cats and the dying mother and screamed to her husband to find an animal hospital to help them. Google results forced them to drive thirty minutes with this family of cats in the backseat. Upon arrival, the receptionist asked a still blubbering Lauren to go to the urgent care center across the street for oxygen, because she was *that* emotionally distraught! The opposite can happen, if you are usually an emotional person. Suddenly, in the face of trauma, you are like a triage doctor—calm, cool, and collected.

What I found to be the best about this transformation is you act differently because you're free of the typical expectations and pressures. It's a little like when old people start having verbal diarrhea because they don't give two shits anymore about offending people or telling people what they want. They've lived a lifetime, and toward the end, they have somewhat figured out what is really important in life—and maybe today it's important to let you know that they think your kid looks a lot like Howdy Doody, or that your new haircut reminds them of the helmet Marvin the Martian wears, and do you really need to eat that crepe because it looks like you don't know where the gym is. Yup, just like this, pregnancy can free you. You, too, have finally figured out what matters in this lifetime—the health of your unborn child—so you don't worry so much about your appearance, re: weight and perfection, or what your boss thinks of you, or if you forgot to send a birthday card to Uncle Carl, because who the hell cares? All you care about is making good decisions for the well-being of your unborn baby. And there's no other way you'd rather be . . . so you finally can drop the act.

> *If pregnancy were a book they would cut the last two chapters.*

—Nora Ephron

Transformation #7: You'll Want a Fetus That's a Genius.

Headphones on belly, mobiles that twirl to Pachelbel's Canon in D, and the complete set of *My Baby Can Read* to take notes to in your last trimester—these are things you become obsessed with when you get pregnant. *No fetus of mine is going to be dumb!* That's the mind-set that put the triple play of brain wave–inducing music—Mozart, Beethoven, and Bach—on the top tier of many a wish list. Never mind that now after the kids have come, I prefer the relaxing piano of Chopin any day, these three amigos along with the most well-known genius—Einstein—dominated my baby registry like an overgrowth of dandelions—seemingly benign, but on second look—completely annoying nuisances.

Transformation #8: You'll Start Preparing the House for Baby in the Form of Cleaning Obsessively.

It's called nesting. You plan your baby blog and move furniture and prewash all of the baby clothes in your lifetime supply of Dreft. You don't procrastinate when it comes to putting together the crib, painting and decaling the room, or writing out thank-you notes for the baby shower you haven't had yet. In six to nine months, you have somehow figured out a way to reorganize your life. All nesting really is is the creation of a semblance of control over a very overwhelming experience—getting ready for baby—so take advantage of the organizational boost and nest away so you can rest away!

What's Your Birth Plan?

Umm, to get this kid out of me! But really, I have to admit yet again, this was another thing I fell for. Women today are expected to have considered another to-do list agenda: devising a birth plan. You and your partner or whoever your "birth coach" will be, i.e., the person on whom you will unleash the beast once labor starts, should have a plan and communicate it firmly to your OB. By the way, your doctor will really despise you when you share with him/her what's in your birth plan, or worse, what's not. "That's not really in our birth plan, Doctor." To which he/she replies in his mind: *Bite me.* This is just a surefire way to alert your doctor to call in sick the minute you go into labor. I've asked a few doctor friends of mine about this, and it's pretty unanimous that they don't like to be told how to do their jobs. For doctors who catch babies for a living, your birth plan is annoying as all hell. Common sense tells me I shouldn't tell the sanitation department how to manage trash, so I'll stay away from micromanaging the guy who went through a million years of med school.

Transformation #9: Books, Videos, Documentaries, and Dr. Christiane Northrup Will Report That Women Can Have "Orgasmic Births" (Yes, an Actual Orgasm While Having Contractions) . . . and Here Comes the Transformation Part: YOU WILL ACTUALLY BELIEVE IT.

The hippie in me wanted to trust that the women on the documentary *Orgasmic Birth* really were feeling aroused and in ecstasy during their contractions, and were indeed having seismic orgasms for the world to see. *All I have to do is not be afraid of the pain?* Well, I wasn't willing to take the chance that my version of an orgasmic birth would be me spitting giant venomous loogies like darts as Brian ducked for cover beneath the bedpans. "Where's the fucking orgasm you promised me! I HATE YOU!"

Transformation #10: You'll Be Asked These Incredibly Annoying Questions and Receive These Unsolicited Comments Over and Over Again.

Do you know what you're having? Because *I* know what you're having!

Do you have names picked out? Oh wait. Are you going to be *one of those* who don't say what the name actually is?

Are you going to breastfeed? Or inhumanely give your child processed food à la formula?

Are you going back to work? If you are, I bet you HAVE to. I, on the other hand, really want to stay home, spend time with my baby . . . bond, you know? It's just not healthy to go back too soon.

Transformation #11: About a Month before You Have the Kid, You Will Freak Out and Insist on Calling the Whole Thing Off.

Toward the end, the novelty and fun of pregnancy wear off, and you are left with anxiety over how the baby is actually going to come out. You hear horror stories, you beg people to tell you everything because you want to know how it will all play out. Personally, I didn't want any smoke and mirrors or anyone telling me that the birth would be a magical experience, unless they meant black magic.

On the other hand, a lot of my friends weren't so much concerned about labor and delivery as they were about the future of their relationships. Soon they would never be alone ever again with their partners, and they'd never know what it was like to go on a business trip without a care in the world. I thought about our Sunday morning rituals, whether it was reading the *Times* in bed or watching *The Today Show* over a pot of coffee. Were Brian and I going to turn into those grimacing couples who wrinkle and sag after a year of not sleeping and who bicker over whose turn it is to do bath time? *Will he start calling me Mommy and, even more awkward, will I refer to him as Daddy? It's just too much to bear. You know what? I've changed my mind. I really just wanted to experience being pregnant, have a few of those naked pregnant pictures taken, like Demi Moore, maybe even have an excuse to read* The Big Book of Baby Names, *but the inability to sleep off a hangover . . . I think I'll pass.* Have no fear, dear reader, biology has its way . . . the real miracle of birth is how quickly you'll change your mind back once you're in labor, bartering anything with anyone to get the damn thing *out!*

The perfect pregnancy does not exist, nor does the perfect pregnant woman. There are hundreds of more things that you will hear, believe, discount, experiment with, and curse while you are going through this miraculous and completely insane time—more than I could ever offer you in this chapter, or in this book. If you don't take the women who perpetuate this bullshit lightly, they will drive you crazy, and tempt you to keep up the act. You know who I'm talking about—the one who competes against the pregnant lady in the OB's waiting room, who boasts about her four-pound weight gain—or four-pound weight loss two minutes postpush—or her $10,000 baby stroller, or the fact that her husband bought her a tennis bracelet for her push present. *Jeez, there must be something wrong with me. . . .*

If I could do it all over again, I'd say it right to her face right there in the waiting room: "Drop the act, will ya? I know you are exhausted because you can't sleep on your left side like the damn books tell you have to, and because you'd rather eat the banana split that you've been jonesing for, and would prefer your husband cry in your lap because he is so overwhelmed with gratitude than to hand you a piece of jewelry."

I'd love to see her face—the relief, the peace in knowing we are thinking, feeling, and doing the same things at the same time. All we have to do is drop the act, help each other drop the act, and validate each other's feelings, thoughts, fears, joys, experiences once and for all.

Who knows, maybe then we can actually enjoy our pregnancies and prepare ourselves *practically* for baby, and love ourselves (and our stretch marks) in the process.

4

The Act: My Baby Can Read! And Other Ridiculous Things You'll Say and Do after Baby

Why to Drop the Act: Because I'm sorry, no baby should read

There is no such thing as a perfect parent so just be a real one.

—Sue Atkins

$\mathcal{B}$ack in 2008, my friend told me she went to a family gathering to celebrate her cousin's baby's first birthday. They marveled over how quickly the year had passed and who would be next in the line of procreation. But the main attraction wasn't baby Sarah. It was what Sarah could do. The family was summoned to the TV room, where they were promised that she was about to mystify everyone. Proud mommy popped in the DVD titled *Your Baby Can Read* and began having Sarah demonstrate that she, in fact, twelve months in the making, could read.

Why? Why are they watching this precious little girl, whose brain still hasn't been able to tell her legs to walk, and who loses controls of her bowels at the sight of DJ Lance (don't we all?), like she is one of Jane Goodall's apes? Why is her mother, clearly still high from hormonal imbalances, encouraging this? Does she hold a deep dark secret of illiteracy, for which she now looks to her daughter to compensate?

This, in a nutshell, is parenting in this millennium, which is being done by parents of the previous millennium, which frankly means they should know better! But instead, it doesn't seem to be getting better. We've heard the countless stories of ludicrous standards put on children via the Common Core curriculum, nursery school application processes that begin before conception, and dance moms who make their girls (and boys) tap-dance until their toes bleed. We push, we prod, we worry about our children being . . . wait for it . . . *average.* Because, by golly, that would make us average, too. So we stress out. Do they know their sight words by age four? Can they read Level G by kindergarten? Can they identify Uganda on a map, and do they know where the Marianas Trench is? And who says the more you learn, the more you know? I can't tell you the amount of shit that I learned in prep school that has literally served me no purpose at all. Clearly, I was never going to be a rocket scientist, so I have yet to put to use the countless geometry lessons. I did, however, thoroughly enjoy my fiction and film class with Mr. Broncato where I read (and watched) *A Clockwork Orange.* Now that's the shit that stuck! Or my all-time favorite, which I still have had no use for—learning about the combustion of gases when heated by fire. Let me tell you what I am not doing in my kitchen: heating combustible gases (I think).

And after kids learn this stuff, it's not enough. On top of all that, we stress out some more. And then when reports about stressed-out children make the headlines, we are completely and utterly taken aback, aghast even! So, in response, we do what seems to make logical sense, when in reality it is indicative of how freaking messed up we are—we give trophies to kids for "showing up," we take them to bowling alleys with guardrails blocking the gutters because God forbid my child learns what a gutter ball is! How the hell could she ever be expected to come back from such defeat? They go to rolling-skating parties where you can rent literally a walker with wheels on it that children push around looking like ballistic geriatric patients (which make scary pictures, by the way), because why should children fall? Well, I ask you, how the hell are they going to learn how to get the fuck back up?! We yell at other kids for calling Richard Jr. "Dick" in the school yard, and then make excuses for Richard Jr. when he acts like one!

So let me get this straight. We sit with our kids and make them do two hours of homework in first grade, but applaud them for missing a goal? Do we have this backward or what? In the world I used to live in, homework was torture and missing a goal was not—well, it was torture but a different kind.

And speaking of. Have you heard about the push to enact the mercy rule in high school basketball? The mercy rule in itself is just another way we contradict ourselves. The overtesting and overteaching kids pushes them to compete against others who might be naturally better in school, or better yet, simply better test takers. Then we take our kids' scores, pit them against other kids, compare them to the results of other schools, and then what? Label our kids based on whatever arbitrary number happened to land on their third-grade test that year. I have one question: Where's the fucking mercy?

Take a basketball team, who most likely is mismatched to play another team, have them not be as good at basically anything to do with a ball, a basket, and a court, and stop the game when they are getting an ass whipping?

Look, I was an athlete all of my life. I loved the feeling of being on a team, I loved the energy and frustration I could healthily take out on the field, and I certainly loved to win. But with winning, I learned how to lose as well. Here's a philosophical question: If you lose 101–2 or 101–100, don't you still lose?

Malcolm Gladwell made famous the rule of ten thousand hours, explaining that in order for someone to get good at something, he or she must commit ten thousand hours to the subject matter. Regardless of if a team sucks or is amazing, they only stand to gain from putting in more hours. Now, the other side of the debate says that coaches are "running up" scores and purposely pummeling less talented teams. But, in college sports, this tactic is actually welcome. It helps rankings and it also helps the stats of players for any scouts who might be looking for them. So here is another ludicrous contradiction. Common Core was implemented with the specific goals of making kids "college and career ready." Okay, so how does asking for mercy in high school prepare kids for the big bad world of playing the sport in college? There is no mercy in the real world. The last time I checked the account executive who lost the advertising account to a kickass campaign didn't ask for mercy in the boardroom. "Please stop running circles around me with your brilliant ideas, have mercy."

Drop the act. Instead of teaching children to ask for mercy, match the teams better and teach sportsmanship to the winning team, who might on their own accord take it down a notch come third period. I mean, what kind of message do you send to the team that's doing well? "Don't give mercy until they ask for it"? A little harsh, don't you think?

Or, the coach could take a knee with the team and explain that the rest of the game, they are going to observe the other team and what they are doing and how they are doing it. Yeah, that's right, turn it into a learning experience.

We cannot claim our kids to be amazing readers by age three and then have the audacity to protect them from being plain awful at a certain sport. It just doesn't add up. And really . . . where the hell would Hollywood be without the concept of being killed by the opponent? *Major League*, *A League of Their Own*, *Rudy*, *Cool Runnings*, *Remember the Titans*, the goddamn *Karate Kid*! From my recollection, none of us lined up to see *The* Good *News Bears*!

In my opinion, parenting is not something that is compartmentalized. Dropping the various acts we've picked up along the way in the parenting realm can help us remember that *everything* is an opportunity to grow our children. Sports and life are related, as art and life are, business and life, and on and on. We are the sum of all our parts. What we do on the field very much affects what we can do in other areas of our lives. Teaching kids to do their best on the field and look for ways to learn from others is a metaphor for everything else. Teaching them to ask for mercy? Same metaphor.

I came to parenting the way most of us do—knowing nothing and trying to learn everything.

—Mayim Bialik

Then come the studies saying that children are more depressed, mean, isolated, antisocial, and we question why it is like that? How about questioning ourselves? Didn't we play a part in creating this monster problem? What happened along the way? Why is he so screwed up when he knew where Uganda was before he knew where his penis was? Hmm. Maybe a small percentage of it has to do with our tendency to relentlessly push children toward developmentally inappropriate things while pulling them away from the character-building opportunities like striking out in baseball!

Stop the act! It's exhausting you, *and* more importantly, your kids.

Your child will read, and you know how she'll learn? Through her being curious about what something says. She'll become frustrated that everyone else around her knows where the bathroom is or what theater the movie is playing in and she doesn't. She'll, by the good grace of peer pressure, *want* to read, on her own volition. That's what kids do, that's how their brains are wired. That's why they're so much better than us grown-ups. Drop the act, and let's stop dragging them down to our sorry levels.

However, if you're still interested in having your child read *Harry Potter* before pre-K, you can check out the DVD collection for about $200.00. (Note: in 2012, the company for this series was shut down and fined by the FTC for fraudulent claims. I know, because my eight-year-old daughter read me the news story.)

More Delusions You Need to Cure after Baby Comes

Once you're a parent, your sleep and feeding schedules aren't the only things that change. If you think you and

There, I Said It! Confessions from the Trenches

I am in a position I am sure many families are in with a child (or children) with anxiety. The sheer notion that she has a test in twenty-four hours, a boy called her a name or some girl she doesn't even like didn't talk to her on any given Tuesday is completely catastrophic to my kid. I find that being really transparent about things is best with her, that honesty is the best policy so that there are no major surprises that she can't handle. I can't imagine what it feels like, for her to live in such a chaotic world. I am the parent who dropped the act and suggested she quit orchestra because she had to get up an hour and a half earlier two days a week. The way I see it, why add more stress to her already stressful life? What about choosing activities that allow them to release some of that stress? What about focusing on one or two activities that they really enjoy and leaving it at that? What happened to being a kid?

It's a hard pill to swallow knowing that the pressures of everyday life are already taking hold on a child by the age of eight. What does that say about parents who can't drop the act and just let the kid play, for fear that their kid might be the oddity? I hope to never add to the already loud noise that she has in her head; I'd rather provide her outlets to let that kid part of her roam wild, while not worrying about a test, a boy, or competing with some overly scheduled classmate that she doesn't even like.

hubby will be able to get it on the same way you used to, well, we need to nip that delusion right in the bud here and now. So many women are hung up acting like they still have the urge or the energy to put out on a weekly basis. Drop the act and stop making the rest of us, who'd rather cuddle up with a good book any day over moving over to our partner's side of the bed, feel ashamed of the cobwebs that might be forming.

It's really hard to get your sex on when you're a parent. Right when you are about to slither your hand beneath the bedsheets in search of your husband, your four-year-old calls, "Mom-meee, I'm done. You can wipe meeee now," in a singsong that you would otherwise think is adorable, *if* you weren't trying to get laid. Somewhere along the line, "You can wipe me now" becomes a warped privilege granted by your little one. More often than not, and especially when I am trying to exercise my right to screw my husband, I wish I would let go of my fear of my daughter's inability to get it all herself, and let her give it a whirl like a "big girl." Like a rite of passage, I'm denying her, à la *Big Daddy*, "I wipe my own ass!" But there's something about parenthood (and I stress parenthood and not just motherhood, because my husband, too, has begrudgingly acquired this paranoia) that makes you obsessed with poo. It starts off in those nifty new parenting classes you and your dumbfounded husband take to learn how to change a diaper, which includes unsolicited information about the child's first turd, called meconium. Think tar. So, no sooner is that kid swaddled and behind the glass of the nursery, you're already waiting for that first poo (like literally praying that it will happen) and the rest is history. The idea of my precious squeaky-clean little girl, in her funky little yoga pants and "Too cool for school" T-shirt, going on with her day with the slightest residue caught all up in her business, is enough to send me on a maniacal on-line hunt for the perfect bidet. It's like something biological that we are compelled to do for the survival of the species: feed them, shelter them, wipe their asses. So, I hand my husband a tissue for his use, while I grab an entire box of wipes and head to the toilet from which my little killjoy's legs are dangling.

Additional to having hackneyed sex, if any at all, you will never again have an uninterrupted conversation—you know, the kind that has a beginning, middle, and an end, an actual point. Talking is for idle fools. You're a parent now, which means you take orders and catch up with your husband in between passing him the grocery bags and calling back your mother-in-law. Things that you know you need to tell each other, important things, like the prospective clients loved the proposal or Aiden got her report card or the oil burner is almost empty, are marked in your head as "Remember to tell Brian . . ." and then something happens that transfers that item from the frontal lobe to the place in your brain that stores something as memory, and then you actually believe you already had the discussion; because just like smoking too much Mary J, your brain just doesn't work that way anymore. Kids suck your memory out of your brain, just the same way they steal your sex life!

Later, when the house is freezing because there is no oil to heat the damn house or a bill from the math tutor comes because the report card could have been a bit better, and you started and finished your job with that client, you catch up on the events of the month, albeit, last month, through text message:

Husband: what is this check you wrote for $250 for 2+2=math?

Wife: for the tutor

Husband: what tutor

Wife: I told you

Husband: no you didn't

Wife: do you think it's easy having a full-time job, while doing everything around the house, and booking tutors?

Husband: I'll just write "tutor" in the log

Conversations with any other adult are difficult to have, especially with small children around, because they have this sixth sense that alerts them as to when our attention is diverted from them. I notice this with my little narcissists all the time. I find it highly suspect that at the very moment I decide to check my e-mail, a bloody scene happens in the living room. My friend's six-year-old son once literally screamed at her to "get off the stupid phone," and then when she did, he left the room. And don't even think of getting on the phone with someone who doesn't have kids when those nut jobs are home; that's like trying to speak Mandarin to someone who only understands French.

In the rare instances in which you are actually having a conversation, what normally would be a two-minute anecdote turns into a drawn-out novella, interrupted by name calling, glass-breaking, dog tail pulling, or the old standby, "You can wipe me now." Your funny little ditty is transformed into a really boring, unentertaining story containing rhetorical questions like "Where was I?" and "Oh, yeah, I remember." I noticed that after a few years of such deformed communication, moms just give up and no longer waste precious air time with asking "Can you hold on" or saying "Excuse me"; they just continue telling their story while simultaneously negotiating (and punishing) their kid, or resort to texting.

"So, when the office manager actually told me . . . *goddammit what are you doing* . . . that I need to start emptying my own . . . *get out of the freezer* . . . garbage *I don't care if you fit* . . . I went to her boss . . . *no you cannot have ice cream* . . . and complained . . . *just get out of my sight, will ya?*"

So your husband and you will have to make dates to talk about your day weeks after the day came and went, you and your friends will no longer notice who is screaming at whom, and you'll live in a delusional world in which making a mental note to tell someone something equates to it actually having happened.

It kills you to see them grow up. But I guess it would kill you quicker if they didn't.

—Barbara Kingsolver

If actually believing your baby is literate and your sex life is better than ever aren't prime examples of lying to yourself, here's the "act" I love the most: "I don't need to drink to get through this." If that's so, then why, according to a 2007 article in the *International Journal of Wine Business Research* and a 2009 Nielsen report, women purchase as many as eight out of every ten bottles of wine?

Let's get real, we have all sat in the car in our very own driveways, praying that our husband actually has the kids in bed, only to walk through the door and find they aren't even in their pajamas yet! That's a hit-the-bottle moment, if I ever heard of one! My friends and I laugh so hard about how many times we'll call ahead before deciding to come home from wherever we've been hiding, like the beauty aisle of CVS or the supermarket. When we confirm what we suspected, they are still up, we make a U-turn and get the fuck out of Dodge.

Look, every generation has its "vice." Ours just happens to need wine as much as water. When my girlfriends call before dropping by, they ask, "What wine do you want me to bring? Are we doing white, then rose, then red? Are we just doing white and then graduating to red past 6 p.m.?" We splurge on the first two bottles and then knock off the cheap stuff when we know we won't notice!

We have a full-on strategy. We're professionals. There are even books for moms that center on wine. Trina Epp and Leah Spear wrote a book called *Pour Me Some Whine!* that inspires a celebration of a whole new type of club.

Are You in da Club?

Take this little test to see where you stand, or if you can stand!

1. When your kids are playing in the bath with rubber duckies, do you bring along your own Yellow Tail?
2. Do you avoid signing your kid up for that 8 a.m. Saturday basketball clinic because it will cramp your Friday night style?
3. Do you find you are frequently making meals that require wine as an ingredient?
4. True or False: Wine stoppers have zero function in my house.
5. True or False: If I can only have one glass of wine, I'd rather have none.
6. True or False: I see no point in buying one bottle of wine when my wine rack holds six.
7. True or False: The title "wine store" rolls off the tongue much smoother than liquor store.
8. True or False: It's classier to buy a case of wine instead of one bottle four or five times a week.
9. True or False: The wine store clerk gives my children candy.
10. True or False: I cook dinner while drinking wine rather than drink wine while I cook dinner.

"Pairing wine with a mood, feeling, or emotion can be just as satisfying as pairing it with a great dish," says sommelier Sara d'Amato of winealign.com. Let's drink to that! We know all about moods, and that they don't necessarily come in waves—they can hit you all at once like a tsunami—and dealing with them sometimes requires less talking and more sipping, which is why we pass the vino nightly in lieu of seeing a therapist.

Novinophobia (n.): the fear of running out of wine

Well, now that I've busted your Prosecco bubble and there are no longer any acts to hide behind, how the hell are you going to survive and thrive as a parent? Glad you asked!

Get Yourself a Playdate of Your Own

The first day of school for your child is like the first day at school for you, too. You are walking into a room filled with . . . *gulp* . . . women you don't know! All of those emotions of self-consciousness you felt as a kid walking into school when your so-called best friend was mad at you come flooding back; you have now reentered the school zone. Calling your lifelong friend might be your first instinct, especially because she's been through this before, but I urge you to consider the importance of making a new friend, one who is in your immediate school proximity.

This is really scary because when we are surrounded by women we don't know, it's like the mommy version of "stranger danger." We put our guard up, we look ahead, puff out our chests, and put on a little holier-than-thou act. Let's drop the act. We're all in the same boat, especially the moms whose kids are brand new to elementary school. We don't know the slightest thing, like the etiquette of the car line, or that so many flyers will be sent home in your kids' folders, you'll feel compelled to make a donation to the National Arbor Day Foundation.

The one time I just said fuck it (well, that's sort of a lie because I always say fuck it) and put it all out there, I introduced myself to a mom: "Hi, I'm Beth, and I love to drink red wine." I *meant* to sound crazy and vulnerable, believe it or not, because that's how I find the moms I want to hang with. Hey, we need our own playdates, too, right? Once you issue full disclaimers like that one you'll see that most women really do want to cut the crap and get straight to it. There is a good possibility that this mom may have a child who will be friends with your child for the next twelve years. Damn, you should know right away whether this woman shares some common ground with you, and I don't mean the same freaking handbag.

Your so-called school bestie is an integral part of living amongst families you haven't known your entire life. That mom (or moms) will be your go-to in times of need; you will spend time together as families, be able to text them on a whim without being self-conscious, and you'll see them more than you see your lifelong friends.

Cultivate the relationship as you would with any other friend, and make sure it's genuine from the start. At this age we don't have to be friends with people the way we felt like we did in high school. Now, we can be discerning. Which means you are also controlling who your kids hang out with, for at least the next twelve years, and that's a very good thing. Drop the "my baby can read" act and the other crazy competitive things moms say to each other when they think they have nothing else to talk about. This way you can discover that you can turn to each other with or without the kids to bitch about standardized testing, take turns suffering through bounce house birthday parties, complain about trying to have it all, and love each other for never accomplishing it.

If you have never been hated by your child, you have never been a parent.

—Bette Davis

Ask for Help Because You *Will* Burn Out—Been There, Done That!

Whether you are a parent who works, you don't work and parent, you half work and parent, or half work and half parent... whatever the circumstance, you *will* burn out. This is where your new school mom friend (or the bottles of wine on the discount rack at Bottle King) can come in handy, but regardless, you need to do something quickly about this self-sabotaging act: "If I want it done right, I need to do it myself," or my favorite, "If I don't do it myself, it won't get done."

Cut the crap. We are important, but not that important. Even I, a firm believer in getting shit done, know I can be my own worst enemy when it comes to this act. I'm a Libra, which is the astrological sign that is literally based on the act of balancing. Supposedly Libras (who boast the icon of a scale) are best when they live in harmony, always achieving the perfect balance of life or else we feel off kilter. The problem is when the moon and stars were aligned to create this so-called balance, neither boasted kids, a

There, I Said It! Want to Make
Your Life Easier? Just Say No!

My girls hear the word "no" from me way more than they hear yes, and boy do I hear the wrath of their prepubescent shrieks. Listen, I know how much easier it is to let them get their way. It seems like a no-brainer to give them the iPod in the restaurant and let them get away with another candy bar while you're trying to talk on the phone (and these are just the little-kid things; I am so not looking forward to the real issues). But I really do believe we do children a disservice by always giving them what they want. I didn't hear yes until I went to college and said it to myself. If you give them everything they want, what do they have to look forward to? If they can eat Oreos at midnight in their bed, what fun would it be to do that in college? One of my favorite things to say, and I'm not sure why I feel it is so much fun, is "I really don't care what you want." Oh, just typing it feels so cathartic, because it's so true. I mean, do they care that I really want a buttery nipple shot right about now? Didn't think so.

This is not to say that I don't pick and choose my battles. If it's staying up later than their normal bedtime, okay, fine. But if the things they are asking for are either unsustainable or are not realistic to how one behaves in real life, like not being able to survive short car rides without the entertainment of a fucking song and dance, then the answer is Hell No!

career, a relationship, friends, or a fucking life! They are rock and fire and aren't expected to do much of anything else except stay up there and balance!

I want to scream so many times when I am up to my eyeballs in crap, but instead I tend to just stand there frozen, with my hands on my head, taking deep breaths while chaos is all around me. I say to my girls, "One second" or "Mommy needs a break" or "Mommy *really* needs a vacation" but then alas, I don't take a second, I don't take a break, and shit, what's a vacation? Truth be told (and this book is about the truth), I'm my own worst enemy. Acting as if I have it all together and that it's my sole responsibility to do it all myself is all of my own doing and will lead to my own undoing. How many of you have ever complained that nobody ever asks how you are? It's like gimme gimme gimme, and you wonder if anyone even looks at you as if you are a person. I'm still working on dropping this act myself, but starting now, I am going to be more accountable for how I set up my own traps. What happened to me anyway? I'm not a martyr, am I? From now on, I am going to cut myself some slack and try doing the following to reset my buttons and ask for some more help.

1. Open a bottle.
2. Open another bottle.
3. Open a third bottle and share it with my husband because at that point three bottles deep, I'm in the sharing mood.
4. Spend time with my best girlfriends.
5. Spend time with my guy friends. They shoot straight, are good for laughing at just about any of my jokes while making fun of me at the same time, and most importantly, make me feel like a kid again.
6. Spend time away from my kids, even for a few hours. Absence makes the heart grow fonder.
7. Spend time away from my spouse. Need I say more?
8. Eat a meal alone in a nice restaurant.

9. Write! Write! Write!
10. Be a stoic. Stop and remind myself that I am so incredibly blessed to have this life with a loving family, the best friends ever, and so much love . . . so even when the going gets rough (and we all know it does), I put it into perspective and always think this could be so much worse!

We all need to drop the act and admit that we do indeed need help, our babies are not literate, our husbands are not sex machines, and we are certainly not always feeling like sex kittens, and whatever other thing you put out there to make sure everyone thinks you are the greatest parent in the world. We all have our moments, we all balance a shitload, and we all need a break from our own lives. Let's take the break however we see fit, and then dive right back into the messy lives we lead.

5

The Act: Forty Is the New Twenty

Why to Drop the Act: So you can actually figure out how to accept your body and live life to the fullest, no matter your age or size

Loving ourselves through the process of our own stories is the bravest thing we can ever do.

—Brené Brown

"You don't know what you got till it's gone." That basically sums it up for me when I think about my body. All my life I wanted to be thinner, prettier, tighter. And then I turned thirty-nine. My lifelong friend thought I would be touched by the shadowbox collage she made of the two of us celebrating my "big" birthday—twenty-five—with a note jokingly preparing me for the countdown to my next "milestone." Oh, *that's* what we're calling forty these days? How nice . . . a milestone, like when Brian and I went from dating to engaged. And just like when Aiden went from sitting up to crawling. Or when Lila began hopping on one foot and putting on her own shoes. Milestone, my ass! Unless the "miles" referred to the ones that my body and face looked like they had traveled up till now—weathered, uphill, in the snow—and the "stone," the one I would be using to build the cairn above the grave I might as well be digging for myself.

Normal, well-functioning women, especially all of these "forty is the new twenty" bullshit ambassadors, would look at their past selves and think how far they had come, saying something to Oprah, like, "I'm so happy I'm no longer that naïve little girl who used to be concerned with trivial things like whether the rich, hot Wall Street guy wants to bang me, or whether my *Devil Wears Prada* boss will give me time off for that girls' trip to Costa Rica." But I *didn't* feel lucky in the least to no longer be "that girl." In fact, I wanted to *Quantum Leap* myself into the picture and bitch slap my ungrateful self across her rosy, plump cheeks, the ones I used to loathe because they were so "full." The longer I looked at the picture, the more my eyes burned. All I could think to myself was *What a waste! Why the hell didn't I know how cute I was, and ENJOY IT?!*

The Truth about Youth

"Youth is wasted on the young." George Bernard Shaw said that, and he wasn't even a woman! It's definitely so much worse for us. The propagandists don't agree. They've been banding together for far too long now to spread this PC garbage that we are soooo much happier as we age, perpetuated by even older celebrities who proclaim menopause "the sexy years." I give an A for effort but an

F for accuracy. (By the way, I realize this is no longer the current grading system, which really doesn't help me feel any younger.) Old Georgie knew it: youth is to be pined for, longed for. Youth is where it's AT!

At twenty-five, I was walking around, the embodiment of gravity's bias toward youth, and I was totally clueless. As I took a closer inspection of the shadowbox, I reached for my reading glasses, which is just a nice way of saying magnifying glass, hoping they would help me remember myself as I was in that moment. I accepted the fact that the girl in the picture *was* me. She did sport my favorite hoop earrings of the era (which is still my signature look), but I couldn't get inside her head, which frustrated the hell out of me. How could I not relate to my own self! It's as if fifteen years equals one human life. Like dog years, except in midlife dogs don't find their nipples aiming for their knees.

The only thing I could remember about that girl in the picture, who was raising a cosmopolitan, embracing her inner (and outer) Samantha, was that she was overly concerned about her weight, despite how insanely taut her underarm skin was; my boobs were closer to my neck, my neck was closer to my chin, my chin closer to my eyelids, which were closer to my forehead. That biased bitch, Gravity; she was still on my side then, high-fiving me: "Your metabolism kicks ass—go ahead, have another beer and burrito supreme from Taco Bell at 4 a.m., after a night of barhopping on High Street."

Fuck gravity.

But look, I can't be all doom and gloom about this, right? RIGHT? I have to get a grip. I have a life, a family, a career, a future. For fuck's sake, I'm a mature woman who has wisdom on her side. Yeah, wisdom! But the problem is that now in midlife (the word makes me physically ill), I don't feel psychologically or emotionally aged. In fact, I think I act more immaturely, only creating an even more wicked contrast to my older physical self. Here I am a mommy who's making an effort to raise two "young ladies" and be all role model-y, still buckling over in laughter when I hear a potty joke.

When I was growing up, grandmas were about fifty; I assumed they were preoccupied with all things serious— Son of Sam, Iran/Contra, and who shot JR. Now just a decade away from the Grannies of yesteryear, my own actions reveal that they were just like me: belly laughing over the Jerky Boys, squandering their time perusing beauty magazines, and trying to perfect their blow job techniques. I'm relieved by this revelation. I don't have to feel pressure to change along the lines of the rest of my aging self. Now, however, I'm left with the inevitability that one day I'll wake up and not recognize myself in the mirror.

A colleague of mine told me the story of her grandmother, who has a touch of dementia, who told everyone she had made a new friend, and that this friend did everything she did. Turns out, the new mimicking friend was her own reflection in the mirror. This ninety-year-old woman didn't recognize herself, or perhaps didn't want to recognize herself! I think we all can relate to some degree. Ever been at the department store and catch a glimpse of a woman in one of those columns that doubles as a mirror and think to yourself, *At least I don't look like her*, only to shudder at the realization that it is fucking *you*?! Well, if you haven't, you will.

The worst part is, the "forty is the new twenty," and the "sixty is the new forty," peeps don't really address how awful it is that you no longer get served at a bar right away! The invisibility factor will happen, and if we are not prepared, we won't handle it with poise and will continue waiting far too long for a damn glass of wine! So what do we do? We continue to go on diets, count our carbs, try to live gluten-free lives, buy a Groupon for hot yoga—which we secretly hate, but do anyway—all in the name of longevity. Long live the act.

I'll be honest, I am my own star of this particular act. I do all of it as a defense against becoming a fat sow and hating myself while applying my new "age-defying" liquid makeup and working on the subtlest signs of crow's-feet and suddenly disappearing eyebrows, cursing the cigarettes I smoked in college because those lip lines everyone talked about, well . . . they're real.

Do you want to hear something sick? All the women I talk to, when they think about the pre-Y2K versions of themselves, they hardly say longingly, "Oh, to have my whole life ahead of me." They say, "Look at my skin!" "Holy shit, I was so thin!" Followed always by, "What the hell was I wearing?" Nothing about the person we were, how nice or mean, how rich or poor, what a winner or a loser? Nope, it's all about appearances.

That's screwed up.

And if our obsessiveness over what we look like instead of what kind of human beings we are isn't enough, what really pisses me off is that collectively as the female race, we do it to find a mate and impress other people.

If anybody even tries to whisper the word "diet" I'm like, "You can go fuck yourself."

—Jennifer Lawrence

We tend to lambast the media, blaming it, and yes, there is a fault there, when they are constantly highlighting the newest fad diet every celebrity is on, or showing photos of red carpet must-haves including a bandage dress for $3,000. But it's not just the images of the Real Housewives and Katy Perry or *Vanity Fair's* "Hollywood" issue that compels us to more emphasis on cleavage than, say, our vocabulary. Let's take some responsibility for our actions, taking two hours to get ready for our neighbor's jewelry party. Every woman knows we dress for each other. We want to keep up or outdo everyone else. This starts from a very young age.

For instance, at the end of high school and into my first year in college, I became preoccupied with my weight, to the detriment of my health, for one, because everyone else was doing it, and two, I was already an oddity. To my defense, I didn't feel at the time that I had much to stand on in terms of being accepted for myself, as I was one of the only non-super-rich, biracial girls in a sixty-mile radius, and often felt like the local anomaly, a "vanilla and chocolate swirl" (to quote Crazy Eyes from *Orange Is the New Black*) to gawk at. I, too, wanted to wear the clothes my so-called friends wore, deny myself the body my heritage insists I occupy, and wear knee-length leather and suede skirts without having them crease at the thigh or make a moon pie out of my ass, so I went along.

You know that girl in high school who reached celebrity status because she worked at CVS and got employee discounts on everything except cigarettes and chewing tobacco. Every payday, she'd spend half her check on boxes of weight-loss bars in every flavor from peanut butter to vanilla crunch to chocolate fudge. She'd share with her friends the over-the-counter diuretics, appetite suppressants (in pill and gum form), and laxatives (also in pill and gum form). And this wasn't even during prom season—when the free-for-all really began. Girls would skip meals, overload on water, and beeline to the gym after ninth period for what looked like circuit training on crack. Or the girl who would get too dizzy to drive home after her binge workout and crashed her Bimmer—all in the name of looking good in taffeta. I wish I could go back to that poor girl and explain that no matter how skinny she got to be, she was going to look like an idiot regardless, since there is no diet or miracle cure for bitches in shoulder pads!

Because I've been in the media industry for so long, I see nothing has changed. These teenage girls who flirted with eating disorders, swinging from binge disorders to exercise bulimia to waves of anorexia, are now all grown up, and, as the saying goes, old habits die hard. In fact, according to David Herzog, MD, director of the Harvard Eating Disorders Program at Massachusetts General Hospital in Boston, eating disorders are nowhere near a teenage epidemic. A staggering increase in anorexia and bulimia has now been reported in women who are trying to lose pregnancy weight or who have started gaining weight in menopause, or who were never cured of their thirty-year eating disorder in the first place! The damage supermodels caused to our teenage minds doesn't just go away simply because we are older and are supposed to be wiser. Remember, emotionally we'll never be as old as our bodies!

If you ask mothers-to-be why they want to breast-feed, the number one reason is for the health of their child. Do you know what the close second is? To lose weight faster. Which by the way, in my experience, the jury is still out on. (Yeah, you burn five hundred calories every time, but you become a ravenous crazy person and wind up taking in many more calories than one snack should allow!)

So now we have a generation of aging women, who are also still trying to lose weight, but have the added pressure of watching the steady formation of jowls and eleven marks that brand them "tired and used up" right between the eyebrows. We're adults now, but we haven't moved very far beyond the insecurities of our youth, except we aren't afforded the excitement of going to prom.

Admittedly, I am still incredibly body conscious and have worked out six to seven days a week for as long as I can remember; with the exception of during pregnancies where I took it back a bit and aimed for four to five. I had a freaking treadmill in my room in college. The starvation method landed me in the hospital and then visits to an eating disorder specialist and therapist who required me to miss some time at college. The first thing I thought of after I found out I was pregnant was how my life would change, the second was hoping the baby would be normal (a feat, considering . . .), and the third was the fear of being fat for the rest of my life. After I had my first daughter, Aiden, I fought tooth and nail to bounce back, and it took about four to six months; I mean shit, I had a store opening in LA, and I was not going to roll out on the red carpet looking all busted up. But the joke was on me, because after I had Lila, it took two fucking years for me to even get motivated, and then a third year to get back into somewhat of a condition that would remind me of the original me.

Look, I realize this dilemma on how we feel about our bodies, how we feel about aging, and how we feel about society, and treatment of women who are old and/or ugly, is not a new one. I'd bet that the stories above are scarily familiar to most of you. And that brings us to, how do we deal now? How do we drop this act, which has been long in the making, and which we have taken with us into our adulthood? I've looked around and there seems to be two camps: the "I'm going to fight it tooth and nail," and the "What does it matter, no one's looking at me anymore anyway." I say, the answer is somewhere in the middle and can be achieved with preparation and acceptance.

Mitigating the Fear

In therapy there is a type of treatment for anxiety, PTSD, and related disorders called exposure therapy, in which people, provided a safe environment, face and control their fear by being exposed to what scares them. While I am in no way comparing the negative emotional effects aging has on women to PTSD or any other psychological issue (although I would believe it if someone with credentials said it), there is something to learn from facing the music. Knowing what is going to happen helps us mentally prepare and visualize how we can handle it, whether it is by calling in some reinforcements, or letting go gracefully. So, let's rip this bitch off like a Band-Aid, shall we?

> You're 30: You know stuff now. Your 20s were for "ducking up," as my auto-correct would say, and learning from those mistakes. (For instance, never again will I convince myself that sleep is for sissies and go straight from a party to the airport. You will not "sleep on the plane"; you'll vomit in the security line. Go to bed.)
>
> —Olivia Wilde

According to *The Merck Manual*, a change in vision is often the first undeniable sign of aging. Been there, done that. And it's all downhill from here. . . .

Generally, when people are in their fifties, the ability to taste and smell begins to slowly diminish. (Try as I may to imagine this might be helpful with my propensity for wine, optimism fails me. As people age, taste buds on the tongue decrease in sensitivity, affecting our ability to taste sweet and salt while keeping our buds sharp for anything bitter and sour. (Mystery to the plethora of sour balls in nursing homes solved!)

As people age, the gums recede. Let me tell you, I just had to talk a friend of mine off the ledge after she returned home from the dentist for her biannual cleaning. Just one week after her forty-second birthday, her doc said she had receding gums, which exposes her teeth to food particles and bacteria. He gave her a test called a "gross debridement," which really knocked the wind out of her. I mean, the name alone . . . She discovered her tooth enamel was wearing away, and was asked whether her yellowish teeth ever bothered her enough to consider whitening. An hour and $250 later, my friend was Steve Harvey's twin. By the way, whitening one's teeth (not that I'm opposed to it, because my friend's teeth look *amaze*balls) wears away at tooth enamel. Do you see where I'm going with this?

With aging, the nose tends to lengthen and enlarge, and the tip tends to droop. I included this one because I have no idea what to make of it, but I do wonder if it has anything to do with the loss of smell (hmmm), or is it simply something else to prove that nothing is immune to aging? You had me at droop. . . .

Thick hairs may grow in the nose and on the upper lip and chin. The good news on this is, I have had the luck of dealing with hair since puberty, so I feel pretty equipped to handle this one. I am enraged, however, at the irony of having extra chin hair while the eyebrows begin to thin, requiring penciling à la Phyllis Diller.

The skin tends to become thinner, less elastic, drier, and finely wrinkled. You see here is where I beat those bitches from the dog days of growing up. There is half of me that will age slower than the other half of me, thanks to the African American gods who have blessed me with darker pigmentation. I am hoping with all hope that the African American side of me will battle it out with the Caucasian side of me, and win! I am praying that the "Black don't crack" saying holds true for at least *most* of my "older" years. #nofilter, just sayin'!

It can be pretty hard not to gain weight starting in your forties, and you can blame the drop in estrogen. Loss of estrogen sucks, man. It can wreak havoc on our hair—prompting us to secretly research antibalding creams and Kim Zolciak's line of wigs (*blech!*)—make sex painful or nonexistent, and give us night sweats to the point of having to change our pajamas in the middle of the night. You can also look forward to becoming itchy in places that should never be scratched. And I thought gravity sucked. Estrogen is its evil twin, and they should both go drown in a pool of lube.

But the most obvious sign of aging is something that I noticed from stalking Instagram. It's there, but under the surface—the thing about the latest picture posts that seems so different about that person, but you can't quite put your finger on it. I feel slightly ashamed (not much) to admit that this front seat to everybody else's diminishing youth is, well, sort of . . . comforting. I can handle the threat of a thickening waistline, the occasional chapped ass, and the need to focus more on hair replacement than that guy from the Hair Club for Men who is also the president. But here is what goes away that seems to be universally plaguing women of all races, ages, and income brackets—the glow. That's right, the glow is gone. You know, the one that you see in pictures of You, Versions 1.0, 2.0, and 3.0? There is this luminescent aura that is naturally there and it seems to be radiating from the apples of the cheeks. We used to call it "oily skin," but it wasn't! It was youth, and orgasms, and not worrying about remembering to pay the water bill. No matter how much Oil of Olay we slather on, the glow just goes. . . . To me, the lackluster look that paints the face of women of a certain age is as much a telltale sign of true age as the, dare I say, hand test.

What Do We Do?

I must say I am impressed with myself, as I think I have sufficiently outdone my talent for depressing people. But don't be too hard on me; it's all in the name of good therapy. We can move on now because it's done, it's all out there (actually it was a carefully curated list, because the full story is much more macabre). Now, I can't say I have the answer to "now what?" but I do find it helpful to remember this act that we are buying into in the name of youth is really a large bullshit game of manipulation. They *want* us to care! They *need* us to care! They want us to wallow in self-pity and partake in magical thinking that we can actually beat Mother Nature. They plan for us to stop off at Walgreens for toilet paper and Tylenol PM only to leave with $75 worth of pro-retinol serums! They want us to believe that twenty-five-year-old boys can become

There, I Said It! Let Go of Your Irrational Attachment to Your Fucking Hair!

I cut my hair for the first time (in terms of taking off great lengths) at the age of twenty! It was incredibly liberating, and I looked hot! I actually had it short for years, and then like every other person who gets married at the Plaza in NYC I grew it long again for my wedding. Then before I let the ink dry on my marriage license, I cut it off again. This has been a cycle for me for God knows how long. I recently cut it all off again and am now in the process of growing it just a bit to add bangs. WTF! It's the one thing I can control, still feel really good about myself, and know that not everyone can wear so many different hairstyles . . . but I can! It's the part of me that says screw you to everyone, I have it in me to make a change, especially a drastic one! And I don't have to ever risk being that old lady with long hair, or the lady with crappy hair who just would rather it be ass long than ass hot. I know you know what I'm talking about!

If you have unruly hair that constantly makes you look like a disheveled mess, or worse, a mental patient pumped full of Thorazine on *Shutter Island*, cut it off! And please, if you have naturally dark hair, don't get highlights! To look good is to feel good, and you want to look fabulous, so drop the act of trying to pass yourself off as a sun-kissed blonde when your genes clearly say otherwise! The act is no longer useful. It's about to destroy you! Can we find a happy medium where we do a few things to keep our shit up to par? Yes, but sometimes that means cutting the locks. Just because you have the same long "messy" look as one of the Jenner girls doesn't mean you are as young as them.

obsessed with our sexiness, as long as we self-tan, dye our hair, and put in hair extensions, because nothing says "fertility" like long locks. I don't know what to say, other than "I'm mad as hell, and I'm not going to take shit anymore." Time to drop the act, rewrite the lines.

> *The thing about 50 is that you've clearly reached a point where you have more of your life behind you than ahead of you, and that's a very different place to be in. You're thinking, "I've done most of it." I don't like that feeling. But it makes you evaluate your life and go, "Am I doing what I want to do? Am I spending my time the way I want?"*

—Julianne Moore

Time for a Mind Shift

Did you know that when it comes to running, the most competitive category is "Female, ages 40–44"? Of course, this makes sense. Women in their twenties are nursing hangovers on Saturday mornings or enjoying some morning sex; women in their thirties are home nursing their kids (as well as their hangovers) and are too tired to turn the TV clicker on, much less run a 5K. So that's where the free and forty-something set comes in. What I really admire about these women and organizations such as Run Like a Mother is that they are helping women redefine themselves, maybe even run for the first time in their lives, and shift the focus from what they look like or how young they are, to what they are capable of accomplishing. And running is a great metaphor for what happens when we drop the act because running is all about competing with yourself, setting or beating your time goal, or graduating from a 5K to a 10K to a half. That is so refreshing, since we women so often fall into traps of comparing ourselves and one-upping the woman sitting next to us on the train. I'd love for women to let go of the exhaustion they have accumulated after years of secretly wanting to beat out the other assistant for a promotion, hating their dick (or bitch) of a boss and vowing to steal his/her job as soon as he/she hits the wall, using social media to spy on the ex's new conquests, gaining the least weight out of all of their preggo friends (to prove what, I'm not sure), being the most successful working mom of the group. . . . Oh God, I just can't even go on! It's so pathetic!

What I hope is we can all get to a place of looking back at how much time and energy we have wasted pitting ourselves unnecessarily against each other, only to wind up in the same place anyway—at an age and stage where the true competition comes to bear: the one we have with ourselves. Are you going to cower or kill? Choose to enable and perpetuate the act by going on and on about fighting your age and doing desperate things like hanging out with your teenage son's friends (my God, go rent some MILF porn!) and you will still find yourself running under a rock and hiding. The "I'm going to fight age to the core" mind-set *will* backfire. Choose to come face-to-face with your present self in all her unglory (all while making some tweaks so you don't go totally postal when you look in the mirror); you might discover you can't handle her because she's actually stronger than you ever were. That's kinda hot.

I'm not saying go and join a runner's club when you'd rather have a yeast infection than ever run up the block, but do take a lesson from the spirit of doing something that keeps the onus very much on oneself, and actually helps grow you as a person. And isn't that what we're really after here? Growth. Madonna or even Taylor Swift might call it reinvention. We love the memory of ourselves, but why turn our backs on the needs of our future selves? That's so cold. Your present and future self need you! What we do when we allow the act to get in our way, and we refuse to embrace our age or even our bodies at our age, is deny ourselves the opportunity to get acquainted with the new version of ourselves. Too bad for us. She might be really cool, much funnier than when she was twenty, and less stressed, thanks to her internalizing life's most undeniable fact, "This too shall pass." We, as women, are resilient as all hell, but we are self-sabotaging by building our brick wall and placing it right in front of our faces. Smack. Our loss, really. Don't let your present and future self be the "one who got away." She has a lot to teach you, and while you might not think this is comforting in the face of crow's-feet and botched Botox, you'll really never know until you try her out for a spin. Think:

How do you want to look?
How do you want to feel?
How do you want to spend your time?
How do you want to be remembered?
And run with it!

How Do I Love the New Me, Let Me Count the Ways. . . .

We can pretty much Photoshop any flaw away, which I think is why aging is especially difficult for us in this day and age. I mean do we even know how old Jennifer Aniston really is? But what I think is worse than losing our looks is allowing our self-confidence to go with it. Let's face it, that is really what drew people toward us—a certain magnetism that doesn't have to fade just because our youth does. We can get back our moxie!

What we most like about ourselves are the things we *accomplish*. Not things we *have* accomplished or things we *are*. Perhaps, when we're young we are conditioned to want attention for who we are—or a superficial part of who we are. We need to make the mind shift and move toward getting stroked for what we *do*. For *new* things we do.

Maybe that's what I once *did*, but not what I'm *doing* now!

Through researching this chapter, I ran into a post by Marcus Geduld, an English director, who also seems to be quite the empathetic and compassionate cheerleader of aging women. Check out his advice to a woman who wrote to him feeling pretty bad about her thirty-five years. "You need to start seeing yourself as a *process*, not as a memory or as a collection of traits. You are treating yourself as an ossified, finished, fossil that can't be changed or improved."

HOW'D HE KNOW?!

Think back to what you wanted when you were in each decade of your life. My daughter is eight years old, and she wants sleepovers and American Girl dolls. I'm not looking forward to her teens because I know what her heart's desire will be: boys, popularity, cool clothes, and hopefully college. Remember now your college-age years. What did you want? Aside from how you looked and whether or not you rushed a sorority or found your husband-to-be? Weren't you focused on other things besides what everyone thought about you? Maybe you were working on building your resume, applying for internships, looking into graduate programs, networking to find just the right pool of people to offer letters of recommendation. Or if you weren't in college and already working, ambition for the future was a big part of your life. Now that the future is here, how do you want the rest of your decades to play out? I think we should consider our age, our weight today as preciously as I wish we could to our younger versions of ourselves. A fifty-six-year-old mentor of mine, who probably wanted to rip my tongue out and stuff it down my throat for crying about how old I was looking, said to me, "You might feel and look old, but remember you will never be as young as you are right this very second." When I woke up the next morning and realized I had aged from yesterday, it hit me! I finally understood what the phrase "This is as good as it gets" means.

Today, at whatever horrendous age or weight we might be, we will at some point take a picture at some special

---

There, I Said It! That Glow, the One That I Can't Stand Not Seeing in Pictures Is Really the Loss of Mojo

Here is an RX for getting it back without RXs:

Laugh a lot
Eat foods that boost estrogen
Get sleep
Take a cue from *50 Shades*. . . .
Water and wine or, rather, wine then water in that order, because really, wine *is* water
Get rocking reading glasses from warbyparker.com

---

event that we will most definitely look back on in five or ten years' time, and want to *Quantum Leap* ourselves back to our present selves and a bitch slap her for not relishing how amazing she is.

How Do You Know You're on the Road to Accepting Your Age?

Being called "ma'am" no longer ruins your entire day.

You no longer laugh in people's faces after they take a spill and instead, you run to the rescue and help them up, saying, "Oh my God, are you all right?"

You are appalled that your child's classmate just called you by your first name. "Where's the respect?!"

The Super Bowl ends too late, as does New Year's.

You shake your head in disgust over news reports of drinking and driving.

You know where your kid is at 10 p.m.

You can proudly count the years to retirement using only one hand of fingers.

You can take your aging less seriously by laughing about it.

We are always going to want to be the best versions of ourselves, regardless of age, and yes, it is a truth that it's easier to have the best version when you are on the right side of forty. Though we are smart enough to know we can't literally go back to twenty-one, we can live in the moment feeling and looking the best to our abilities. Being preoccupied with age no longer takes over to the point where we miss the moments in life. The goal is to embrace the position we are in, in that exact moment, and have the ability to take it all in. And it's incredibly liberating to concretely make decisions and really stand behind them. When you do it for yourself, and for nobody else, you are no longer acting, literally.

6

The Act: Sticks and Stones May Break My Bones, but Words Will Never Hurt Me

Why to Drop the Act: Because that's complete bullshit! Stick and stones actually *can* break my bones, and words will forever hurt me!

If you judge people, you have no time to love them.

—Mother Teresa

*J*udgment is no joke. We have all been judged in a myriad of ways, and each time feels worse than the time before. Judgmental people coupled with our own terrible habit of harshly judging ourselves directly relates to the epidemic of low self-esteem in women. In fact, judgment is the reason we adopt various "acts" in the first place. We hope our acts act as soothing ointments that cover up the boo-boo and take the sting of being judged or labeled as "less"—less pretty, less successful, and less sufficient. In my case, less one color over the other. Ironically, in our culture of "more," we have become lost in our "less."

"It turns out there's an area of your brain that's assigned the task of negative thinking," says Louann Brizendine, MD, a neuropsychiatrist at the University of California, San Francisco, and the author of *The Female Brain.* "It's judgmental. It says 'I'm too fat' or 'I'm too old.' It's a barometer of every social interaction you have. It goes on red alert when the feedback you're getting from other people isn't going well."

"Feedback" is certainly a nice way of putting it. I don't know about you, but especially in today's hypercompetitive world that is obsessed with "breaking news" reports on botched celebrity plastic surgeries, predicting our children's futures based on an arbitrary test score, and convincing us to squeeze into clothing that only prepubescent boys can fit into, this feedback feels a lot like judgment!

A 2001 study coauthored by psychology professor Roy F. Baumeister, PhD, as reported in Aimee Lee Ball's August 2008 article in *O* magazine titled "Women and the Negativity Receptor," proved the idea that "bad is stronger than good": "Bad feedback, bad parenting, and bad experiences are much more powerful than good ones. People remember the bad more vividly, process it more efficiently, and pay more attention to it." I could only imagine what this study would reveal today, being that it is fifteen years later and social media makes it impossible to ignore or even forget the jabs taken at us. We have literally become conditioned to fear what people might say or think, and that's just screwed up.

Diane Keaton once said, "For too much of my life, I was too afraid, too frightened by it all. That fear is one of my biggest regrets." I don't know specifically what Diane is referring to. Seems to me that being in the public eye and in a business where you are open to judgment and criticism all the time is an indication of fearlessness. I think we all go through a period of time when we are afraid. But of what? For me, it used to be a fear of being myself, and what's worse, of even getting to know myself, even just a little. I wanted to fit in and not have my differences held against me, because when you're young, all you care about is what other people think about you. When your world is very small, the opinions of others become really big.

Growing up in Tenafly, New Jersey, I was an anomaly. I had the body type of a half-white, half-black girl—big butt, skinny waist, big boobs—with the hair of a half-white, half-black girl—slightly frizzy brown hair. White girls had Jennie Garth from *90210* to look up to and aspire to, and black girls had Whitney Houston, but there was nobody on TV who looked like Beth; maybe Lisa Bonet for like a hot second but even so. . . . People would often tell me I reminded them of Lisa Turtle from *Saved by the Bell*, but I think it was less that we looked alike than she was the only teenage black girl on TV hanging out with a bunch of white kids. In that way, judgment has always been a theme in my life.

When I hung out with any guy friends, their parents would give me that cautionary look, as if they were counting the days until puberty, when they would make their sons ditch me, because they were to only date nice white girls, which clearly wasn't me. I socioeconomically lived in that world, but culturally and religiously, I was different, but add the fact that my parents were divorced, I was basically a trifecta of shit. So by the time of puberty, when it came to self-esteem and confidence building, let's just say I wasn't off to an auspicious start. Of course, my mother always told me that I could be anything that I wanted to be, that I was beautiful inside and out, that kids are cruel, and that they just say and do things to bring me down. I find myself saying the same things to my own girls now and cringing at the mere fact that we are still having these conversations, that the world hasn't evolved all that much. The old "sticks and stones" rule.

Except words *did* hurt me.

I didn't want to disappoint my mom, who was trying so damn hard to give her daughter the right advice, but inside I was eye-rolling. I mean, my mother was doling out this advice, when she was the one who needed to take a dose of it the most. I knew my mother didn't like herself very much, and frankly I had learned from a young age that it's much easier to be down on yourself than empowered (and this was before the 2001 study). Go me.

From my experience, self-esteem (good and bad) comes in a ripple. First you learn to not like yourself, and then because you have become convinced that you're not likable, you feel worthless. Therefore if you're worthless, then why should you trust yourself? Or your own inner voice and intuition, for that matter? Until, finally, you lose a sense of who you really are (or the opportunity to get to know who you really are) and instead choose to be anyone *other* than yourself. Ah, the insipid act. While your true self is crying inside because someone just hurt you with her words, or you assume you will get passed over for the promotion, or you've been hopelessly waiting for the phone to ring after that awkward first date, you act like it doesn't matter and words never hurt you. And then, you finally become so cynical and pent up and angry that you start acting like the judgmental assholes who started this whole mess in the first place. There's nothing worse than stooping to a level where only low-lifes live. I should know.

One of my daughters has platinum blonde hair. Now, at one time I lived on the Upper East Side, which, for anyone who is not from the tristate area, means there's lots of old money, nannies, dog walkers, doormen, plastic surgeons, yada yada. When I was alone with her, people would think I was my daughter's nanny. At Dunkin' Donuts one morning on my day off, a woman in line with me and my daughter turned to me and said, "You must be the nanny."

Huh?

Number one. *Had* we already been talking, that would have been a complete non sequitur. Number two. *Had* I been my daughter's nanny, it would have been such a meaningless statement to make anyway. Number three. I felt as if I were being judged based purely on the sight of me, and when that happens, I tend to go for the jugular.

"Clearly," I retorted, "*you* must be in line to order a dozen donuts for yourself because you are 450 fucking pounds!" In that moment, I didn't feel bad about it. I was, in my warped, flunk-out-of-debate-class way, trying to make a point. Maybe she was just in line for coffee. Maybe I was able to produce a child by tapping into my recessive gene pool. Both are correct.

As I walked back to our apartment, playing that scene over in my mind, I became insane with regret and guilt. How could I be so mean? How could I stoop so low? How could I be so insecure? How could I be such a poor role model for my daughter? Anxiety-filled tears started to well, and before the first drop could hit my cheek, I ran to Brian. I told him how I was disappointed in myself in a way I hadn't ever been, and then I gave him a play-by-play of what happened, which resurrected my righteous indignation, which then made me cry with guilt again, because I knew what I said was wrong, but then again why *shouldn't* I set her straight . . .

"You're schizophrenic," Brian said. It made me laugh, because I supposed there was some truth to that. On second thought, though, I came to the conclusion that it's not a mental disease, like multiple personality disorder, to boldly speak up and then feel guilty about it; it's simple confusion—confusion about what's right and what's wrong, when we're allowed to get mad, about what's expected or how to act, what our roles are, and how far we should go to protect our egos and mask insecurities. And it's okay to be confused about what to do or what you have done, because let's be real—we are kind of just winging it day to day, taking cues from unrealistic and unreliable sources. And when curveballs, like the Dunkin' Donuts incident, are thrown, sometimes you just don't know if you should swing or get out of the way. But realistically only one of two things could happen: you hit the ball and run the bases, or you get hit.

At Dunkin' Donuts I got hit. But, thank God for that because that's when I knew that I would never use my mouth for bad again. I want my knack to opine to help, especially when it comes to other women who might be a little "schizophrenic" about things, too. So here's my first lesson: *Just get off the line.* Honesty is the best policy, except when it comes from a defensive place. If a judgment is made about you, don't snap back or try to one-up the person. That's when trouble begins. Second lesson: *When you have moments of confusion as I did at Dunkin' Donuts that day, dig deep to see what the source of the conflict is.* It's usually *never* about the dumbass in line.

What it *is* about is how we have allowed judgment to enter our hearts and minds, until we stop liking ourselves, trusting ourselves, and ultimately being ourselves. Aside from our judgment of ourselves, judgment comes from three places, and if we can identify them, we can rectify them.

Judgment from Your Family = Not Liking Yourself

Like so many others, my self-esteem began with my father. Sadly, he judged me on a daily basis, and man, he didn't mince words. But on the flip side, I wouldn't be able to handle judgment today if he didn't test me so often. I literally had to learn how to see through his words and come to see them as meaningless and ultimately not about me at all. When people throw sticks and stones, it's usually all about them and not the recipient, like my outburst in Dunkin' Donuts. So thanks, Dad, for being such an asshole, so I could be such a strong woman today. When my father passed away, I was somewhat relieved, because I didn't have to be bitten by his venom anymore.

And if my father hadn't died, I probably would've just continued distancing myself from him, because being around haters only makes you a hater; clearly I proved that in Dunkin' Donuts.

I believe that every person crosses our path for a reason. I also believe that people come in and out of your life during certain periods to fulfill some need, and when their job is through, sometimes they simply have to move on. This includes the people who gave you the most heartache and grief. Maybe thinking this way is simply a defense mechanism so I don't go ape shit over the time I lost fretting over things my dad said, or the idiots who called me their friend and then backstabbed me, or the energy devoted to giving myself fully to a romantic relationship that left me brokenhearted. I don't believe in much when it comes to religion, but I do believe in the connectedness of our individual energy and spirt, and I like to believe that whether we are shitty or good to each other, it can be a turning point in our development if we choose to make it so. That's what I chose to do with my father. I chose to accept he was not only part of my nature, but of my nurture. And instead of being resentful of him for trying so hard to judge everyone he came in contact with, I was thankful to be able to exercise a muscle that made me more developed and much stronger in the long run. When it comes to family, I hope you can be inspired to drop the act and allow the hurt to hit you; this way next time you feel judged, you'll know how to pull your punches and trust in your worth instead of allowing your worth to be determined by others.

Nobody can make you feel inferior without your permission.

—Eleanor Roosevelt

The Judgment of Friends = Not Trusting Yourself

So then, let's hypothetically assume that my hunch is right, and there are people in your life who you, for whatever insane reason, allow to constantly knock you down, suck your energy with their narcissism and drama, and who want to see you as miserable as they are. You know the person I'm talking about. She's so passive aggressively negative, she can find something wrong with you the second you walk in the door, and it could be anything from your jacket to something you said weeks ago that you can't even remember. Most likely, she's a carryover from elementary or high school, and up till now you never realized what a chore she is to deal with and how draining she is to your self-confidence.

My friend Belinda had a terrible divorce and went through hell to recover from its devastation, so when she met Nick, we were thrilled at how quickly their whirlwind romance turned serious. The first thing she did was call her parents and her brother to share the news, because nobody had been more worried about Belinda than they had been. But when she decided to call Carla, a friend with whom she had an on-again off-again relationship, she made it the last call of the day. That should've told her something.

"You'll never guess what happened last night," Belinda said, trying to fake excitement but really bracing herself for a snarky response.

"What?" said Carla, annoyed that she had to play along.

"Nick and I got engaged."

Silence.

"Carl? You there?"

"Pah," Carla let out a wave of sarcasm. "You have *got* to be kidding me."

"What the hell is that supposed to mean?"

"You know this guy ten seconds and now you're getting married. What a joke."

A decade of responses like this had been enough. Belinda was so completely happy with Nick that it didn't even dawn on her *not* to tell Carla to go fuck herself. Before she got the words out of her mouth, Carla continued, "Well, at least now that you have *someone*, maybe you'll stop drinking so much wine and drunk texting pathetic messages to everyone. So attractive."

Bitch.

Why do we find breaking up with friends who are not friends at all so difficult? What the hell took Belinda so long to get rid of this toxic waste dump of a friend? Again, I think it comes back to the idea that it is so much easier to believe we are lushes and loons than loving and worthwhile of love. If you are past the age of twenty and still have such a person in your life, trust yourself enough to remove her from your circle; or maybe you will be even luckier and she will be the one to remove you. Tell her to her face that you don't want to be her friend anymore, and trust that only good things will happen as a result. It's not enough to passive-aggressively distance yourself until she "gets the hint." This isn't high school. By not telling her how judgmental and hurtful she is, you just keep up the sticks and stones act. Not calling people out on their bullshit is a nonverbal way of condoning these actions. God, I wish I had the strength to do this in my twenties, but at the time I just didn't. There is no way anyone can ever like herself if she is around people like this. Trust your own judgment of people and say bye-bye. And if you don't purposely do it, life has a way of doing it for you, whether you like it or not.

I don't think a lot of women admit this, but being a woman in her late twenties and thirties can be an extremely lonely thing. Whether you are ambitious and climbing the corporate ladder, starting your own business, beginning a family, or flat broke and working four jobs, one thing is certain: you are focused on something major and that major thing has consumed your social life. This is when you'll notice friends dropping like flies, and one day you'll wake up—the girl who had eleven bridesmaids and who outdid the movie *27 Dresses*—and feel like there's nobody around. What I mean by this is, you don't have those three-times-a-day calls with your best friend anymore, and you aren't meeting for happy hour with coworkers on Thursdays at 4:58. You used to go walking at dusk and talk about television shows and go shopping together. Now, you check your social media outlets to see who had their baby or which ex-smoker friend just ran her first half marathon, or who finally passed the bar.

When your boss is on her period or your small business's Q2 numbers aren't strong, or your hands are worn out from rubbing fake tattoos of fucking Elsa on your four-year-old's arms, you go to grab your phone and realize you feel as if there's no one to call. When the things in your life take over and your social life is down the drain, it can be hard to not feel as if too much time has passed to call someone out of the blue. Some friends become text friends, and you feel okay about it. Some friends wind up being so annoyed at you for not keeping in touch that they do break up with you or make you feel extremely guilty or selfish for being sucked into whatever abyss of the month has sucked you in. Your life gets smaller and more insular. I am here to say, that's actually good news.

The weeding-out process begins and some friends stay at the top, some break up with you, some take up too much of your emotional and mental energy, and some friends, whom you might not have considered your closest, somehow become your closest of all. It's interesting to see what a friendship is made of, and the only way to do that is to put it to the test. Not on purpose, but just by living your life, like Belinda did, the best way you can.

The Judgment of Media = Not Being Yourself

I was reading the headlines on Yahoo, appalled by some of the headlines of the lifestyle features: "Need to tone your tummy? Try this tool at home!" "11 Things You Should Never Do Again after 50." How can we not feel judged when it is implied we should be ashamed of any belly fat or that somehow being of a certain age requires women to alter themselves to fit into society, like they'll be allowed to still walk around as long as they play by over-fifty rules? So we adopt acts that the media places in front of us in the form of famous-for-being-famous women and we emulate them, adopting their stupid turns of phrase, like "Oh, that's *so* hot" (thanks Paris Hilton), or make fucking stupid duck faces when shooting their selfies (thanks Kardashians). We all start drinking overpriced Skinnygirl "wine," listen to the same Britney song, and drink the same skim latte. Believe me, for so long, I was a part of this problem, placing products out there for celebrities to be "caught wearing." Why does this marketing tactic work? Because media banks on the fact that women have so little self-confidence that they will act like other people, namely, celebrities, in order to be accepted. Talk about the joke being on all of us!

> *Be a first-rate version of yourself, instead of a second-rate version of somebody else.*
>
> —Judy Garland

Everything is for sale, especially your self-worth. On the one hand, we are taught that we are somebody, and that our feelings matter; however, those notions become increasingly more difficult to believe when outside influences like the media break down some of those thoughts in order to sell us all something. There is no money to be made by empowering others. We don't see the value in building each other up. In fact, most reality television chronicles women breaking each other down. The media shows women judging each other harshly. Who's an alcoholic, a used-up divorcée; who has a Miss Piggy nose, is jealous of a former friend for becoming a gazillionaire; whose husband is clearly cheating on her; who is a gold digger, has ugly kids, is married to a mobster, can't cook, can't write, can't sing, can't can't can't. "Less than" television is what we should start calling it. Maybe it sounds like a conspiracy theory, but you know, when you live in a capitalist society, there is a lot to be lost if a whole helluva lot of people start walking around feeling goddamn good about themselves.

12 percent of women say they have high self-esteem.

—yourtango.com

See, you're far from alone! If enough women would drop the act and let each other know how awful they feel about themselves, then maybe we can collectively join together to bring each other up! You're not alone. Here's some ideas how:

Have compassion for the haters. We all have insecurities, and people who are weak themselves think breaking you down will build them up. Some take pleasure in other people's pain and then take pity on them. It must be horrible to be so miserable that you can find something ugly about a litter of kittens. Remember these people, too, have had experiences, some probably not so pleasant. Remind yourself that they could very well have been treated the same way at home, by friends, etc. That's most likely what was wrong with my father, and he couldn't break the cycle of judgment. Take heart: there will, at some point in their lives, be repercussions for their actions. After all, what goes around, comes around, sister!

Make a mountain out of a molehill. I don't care if you can't find but the smallest thing about you that is positive, find that thing you have to offer and develop it into your biggest strength. Then do the same thing for a friend, or even an acquaintance. It puts me in such a good mood when I give a compliment to a woman in line at the store, or I receive one. And it doesn't have to be about your physical self. If someone is being calm when her child is throwing a tantrum, tell her how you deal with the same stuff all the time, and validate her, instead of looking her up and down like she should receive the Bad Mommy Award.

Have a friend blow some steam up your ass. Who doesn't ever call their friend and say, "Just lie to me and tell me I can do this." To which she always replies, "You can do this." And then you both laugh. Sometimes we just need to hear reassurance, even if you think it's a lie.

Seek help! If you get to the point where every move you make is governed by what other people think, please talk to someone who is unbiased to help you free yourself from the confines of judgment. Maybe reading this book and discovering so many other women feel JUST like you is enough to bring you out of the shadows and see how you can reverse your fear.

Accept your limitations. When we try to be someone we are not, we will most likely fail and in the end not like

There, I Said It! If All Else Fails, Take a Cue from Fräulein Maria

Look, guys have their *Rocky* bell moments that help them psyche each other up for a big challenge. We have *The Sound of Music*. I remember as a little girl watching Maria dancing and side-kicking her way to the Von Trapp mansion, and now as a grown woman, I still love that part, as it's more relevant than ever. Maria didn't believe in herself but had the confidence song to at least get her as far as that gate. After that she had to dig into something real deep and believe in herself. And she got the smoking hot Christopher Plummer as a bangin' bonus!

"I have confidence in confidence alone! / Besides which, you see, I have confidence in me!"

that version of us anyway. Therefore, it must be assumed that if we drop the act, we will stop failing. Accept who you are *not*, even if it hurts, and then ask people who love you to support you as you find the courage to figure out who you really are.

Set obtainable goals for yourself. Why we overachieve is beyond me. We have to lose weight in a few months or meet the man we will marry by the time we are a certain age. We are our own worst enemies with our self-imposed timelines. How about setting a goal that we can actually control and that we are actually capable of doing. Hell, I even like to add things to my to-do list that I've already done, just so I can cross them off! So what! If that's what it takes to boost your confidence, then tick away!

Find role models or mentors. I have a few for different reasons. I have work role models, mom role models,

friend role models. I think the combination of people
helps me to want to propel further, dive deeper into what
I do, not because I want to be like them, but because I
am empowered by women who have found peace with
themselves and found happiness and success because of
it. All of my various mentors have one commonality: they
are all strong, independent fighters who somehow fought
through negativity, and make it their business to spread
positivity.

Welcome some constructive criticism. (It's definitely
something I need to work on, too, but it's so important.)
Just because we can't stand judgment doesn't mean we
avoid criticism. They are two different things, and it's important not to confuse the two. Judgment is blanketed in
hate, while criticism usually comes from a place of good.
In order to improve, you must be able to take constructive
criticism.

When I was a kid, my mother told me if you can't be a good loser,
you can't be a good winner. If you can't take criticism, then you don't
deserve the praise.

—Halle Berry

If All Else Fails, Zip Up Your Armor: Armor Is the New Black

As a former accessories editor for fashion magazines, I
have been on top of every trend since 1980! And for every
one unique type of accessory, there are ten times as many
unique types of people. Some are beautiful and classic, à la
the fur stole; some are simplistic and trendy, like the *Flash-*

dance leg warmer; some try too hard, like overly ripped denim; a few are senseless, like six-inch stilettos; and others are elegant and confident, like a lizard day-to-night envelope clutch. From haters and narcissists to selfish pricks to "martyrs" and plain ignoramuses, sometimes your only option is to make your accessory of choice armor wear.

Let me explain. "They" say every day before you go out there—whether the boardroom, the playground, the sauna at the gym, or in traffic behind a total schmuck—to zip up your imaginary suit of armor to protect yourself from those who want to see you squirm. Armor wear is a metaphor for resilience, and with resilience comes strength. With my big mouth, it's more suitable to zip my mouth before I tell off someone, but I do find that going out into the world with a little extra padding helps deflect the left hooks that people might want to throw me.

Or, if you like, you can kill them with kindness!

7

The Act: You Can Have It All

Why to Drop the Act: Because having it all ain't all it's cracked up to be

It's impossible for women to have it all, if they have to do it all. It is ridiculous! We tried to kill [that saying] off for years. It blames the person instead of the structure.

—Gloria Steinem

I'm writing this chapter on a Saturday morning, feeling as let down as if I were trapped in a cubicle after a margarita-filled Fourth of July weekend. It's not quite how I imagined writers write their morning papers, at least not real writers. I'm not taking mindful sips of my coffee, peering out a picture window looking out to the Sandia Mountains, lamenting over my next adjective. Where I sit is not at all quiet—the local news is on loop, getting viewers all ramped up about impending weather conditions—and I mainlined my coffee hours ago. These days my morning papers feel more like mourning papers. My environment is not quite conducive to "art," or doing whatever it is I'm doing, which will be considered by many to be the antithesis. In my kitchen, two hours into this one paragraph, I'm waiting for my friend to come watch my kids for me so I can get the hell out of here and get some real work done.

If you know the feeling of trying to clean up after a house party, just as your parents are pulling into the driveway, that's how it feels to work and be a mom at the same time. You are constantly playing catch-up, trying to score a hat trick before anyone notices you left your skates in the locker room! It's never comfortable, never full immersion. Just, *Oh shit, dump the Solo cup in Mom's fern and hurry upstairs to pretend to be asleep*; in short, it's a nightmare!

I wasn't supposed to be two weeks behind on EVERYTHING, and I wasn't planning on biting my mother's head off when she called me to ask if I "had a chance to go to that place to pick up that thing" for her, but last week the school called two snow days, which means the girls were home with me—inside, windows and doors shut, no air, no sunlight. I felt like a nursery school version of the Gimp. In award-winning motherly fashion, I did what anybody who has a shitload of deadlines would—plopped my girls in front of a marathon of American Girl movies. But even the promise of binge TV along with no-strings-attached refills of popcorn and chocolate didn't work, as my girls are still at the age where they need to announce every five seconds that they have to pee or they want a snack or that they are about to beat the shit out of each other. With each hour that passed, and each interruption, and each deadline pushed to the next day, my stomach would sink lower, lower, lower, until I figured out how to soothe myself with lies: *When Brian gets home from work, I'll head off to Starbucks and work for four hours like a maniac. Yeah, that will be even better. This way, I can give*

100 percent to the girls now, and then give my work the 100 percent it deserves. Don't freak out. The day is not dead.

When it comes to Brian, there's no question that he is supportive of me to a fault, but in order to conjure up that support, I need to send subtle messages letting him know how desperate I am. Like, standing with my face peeled to the front screen door, because doing that is my magical way of making his car pull into the driveway faster. Or, huffing and puffing while I read my e-mails at the dinner table, while he tells me how tired he is after *such* a long day, to which I think to myself how much I do not give a shit. To his defense, I usually wait much too long to solicit his help, and that means I am by now a raving bitch. I blame my procrastination on a delusion that I can usually handle 1,001 things coming at me, until I am buried under rubble unable to breathe.

Tonight's subtle message is me being already in my coat and hat, laptop bag in hand, and Lila half-undressed. He's on bath and bedtime duty, and Mama is getting out of Dodge. Warming up the car in the dead of winter when the rest of the world is getting ready to warm their feet in their fuzzy memory foam slippers, I feel more unmotivated than ever. I'm too tired to work, let alone create anything. I push the self-defeat down with an interesting thought: the last time I was out at this time of "night" by myself and not expected to come home for hours was in college, when I was sleeping with someone and didn't want anyone to know. Which brought me to the next logical thought: When was the last time I had seen a movie inside of a movie theater? Nobody would know if instead of going to work on work stuff, I caught the 8:05 showing of *Gone Girl*. And it was a book before it was a movie, and I'm writing a book (kinda sorta). But even my best rationalization can't work around the fact that I am way too fucked with work to really turn this Fandango Fantasy of mine into a reality, so I order my Starbucks half-caf venti skim latte, because coffee at this hour would wreak havoc on my old-lady stomach and my even older-lady sleep cycle. I sit at a table (unlike real writers who would be committed enough to have their favorite table) and spend far too many minutes settling in. The day is not dead. I'm in the here and now, and I'm going to bang this shit out, kick ass, take names, do it all, and do it well.

I look at my notes, remind myself of what I wanted to say about careers and motherhood and living your passion. Oh, right, here I am at "how lucky I am to be a woman in this day and age and to be setting an example for my two daughters so when it comes to them living in their own day and age, they will remember how Mommy had it all." Then the phone rings. Brian.

"Babe, do we have a thermometer that works?"

"What do you mean?"

"Lila feels warm, but I can't get a reading on this damn thing."

"Are you putting it in right?"

"It's not brain surgery, Beth. Maybe she just needs to hold her tongue down longer."

"You're putting it in her mouth?! You stupid asshole. It's a rectal thermometer!"

"What the fuck, Beth!"

"Me, what the fuck? You, what the fuck?"

Fuck.

I slam shut my laptop, chuck my phone in the trash can and throw the whole half-caf in my purse, and remember why a deadline is called a deadline.

There's a haunting scene in the movie *Baby Boom*, which I seem to coincidentally catch every time I turn on the TV on a Saturday afternoon. It's the moment when Diane Keaton, a.k.a. the Tiger Lady, a high-power superexecutive, lets go of the thread from which she's been hanging after a few sleepless nights nursing her baby's flu. The cramp in her lifestyle the baby has created chased Diane's boring boyfriend away, but adding insult to injury, the night before a big meeting that was supposed to make her a partner, Diane gets sick as well. In an overwhelmingly relatable moment, the Tiger Lady leans against the wall in her hallway, dropping her report, which meanders to the floor as defeated as the character herself, a proverbial surrender flag.

I remember watching this movie for the first time, being only a teenager, but still, the scene branded itself in my memory. It spoke to me, but I didn't know yet what it was saying; I just knew that it meant something. It was as if the message was in a different language, not one I would be fluent in until I, too, became Diane Keaton (sans the suspenders and gloves, of course).

You know, we've been fighting the Mommy Wars and debating on what lifestyles are better for our children, women, relationships, the future of the world, and nothing has been accomplished. The Mommy Wars, in my opinion, was a missed opportunity for a societal self-examination. What went wrong was they became less about self-examination and more about self-defense. Instead of asking and answering questions about one's own quality of life and mental well-being, and overall satisfaction, it became an exercise in sticking up for one's choices (even if one was not proud of them), for defending the good fight the feminists who came before us fought, or bellyaching

about whose situation is direr than the other. Finger point-
ing and judgment got out of hand and turned women away
from each other, helping them understand each other
less. I'm no Sun Tzu, but if you ask me, that's the old
divide-and-conquer strategy. Take an incredibly powerful
segment of the population and break it down in one fell
swoop by pitting sides against each other on an issue that,
for the most part, isn't an issue at all.

The real question is threefold. Why have women been
told they can have it all? And why is having it all the brass
ring to reach for in the first place? Is having it all meant to
be a positive thing?

A fish out of water can't live on land. Poor fish, doesn't
know what it's missing.

A man cannot know the sense of accomplishment that
comes from chasing down a cab in stilettos. Good. The
asshole doesn't deserve to.

A woman cannot really relieve an itch the way a man
can relieve an itch on his balls. Nothing can compare (so
I hear).

A turtle can't feel what it's like to soar over the tree
lines.

Eagles don't know the cool sanctity of sleeping in mud.

Maybe it's just me, but if I were a flying fish, living on
land, scratching my balls, and sleeping in cold mud, I'd be
pretty confused and pissed off. I don't think being able to
do all of those things necessarily leads up to anything positive. Yet there are women who would say, no, argue with
every hostile fiber of their being, that this is the complete
picture of happiness.

I can't and I don't. It sucks when you've worked really hard for
certain things and you have to give them up because you know that

you're going to miss out on your child's upbringing, or you realize that your relationship has suffered. I can't direct right now because I would miss out on my daughter. It was heartbreaking to let it go, but it was a clear choice.

—Drew Barrymore

YOU CAN HAVE IT ALL!

It sounds like one of those crazy teasers a ringmaster yells outside a traveling circus camp: COME AND SEE THE BEARDED LADY!

Which, by the way, is more likely than having it all.

Why am I so cynical? Shouldn't I by way of my age, sex, and race, be the poster woman for having it all? I am woman, hear me roar? Technically, born in 1975 makes me the daughter of the feminist movement of the sixties. I mean, even my boomer mother was progressive for her time: a white debutante from the Midwest who married a black man from Harlem? Pretty evolved shit. I'm cynical and a little angry at all of this You Can Have It All stuff because I think it does a disservice along the lines of one of my other least favorite sayings, "You can do anything you put your mind to." It leaves a generation of children who grow up ill prepared for reality.

When I got pregnant with my first daughter, Aiden, there was no question in my or Brian's mind that my career would still be a priority. Nothing at all would change. Why should it, after all? Nothing was expected to get weird for Brian or the track he was on, and we were from the generation that knew just having a vagina doesn't disqualify me from seeing my career goals come to fruition. We'd get full-time help, as in a nanny, and I'd pull my seven to seven, mostly eight to six thirties, and still get to the gym.

We'd make it work, like all modern-day yuppies who find themselves caving to the biological urge to procreate.

Now, let me step back here, and just qualify what I'm saying for those who will read only the words on these pages that they want to (hi, Ma) and determine an entirely different meaning to my message and then post really nasty, hateful blog posts about me. I am not saying you shouldn't work and have kids. I'm not saying that you shouldn't quit your job to have kids. I'm not saying you shouldn't not have kids at all, if that's what you want. I'm not saying that work is not mandatory because of the expenses of life, and this is not about determining which lifestyle is better or who can do what, when, with whom, or without whom. This is simply a question of the bill of goods we've been sold AGAIN, and why the hell we are constantly being targeted for such propaganda. All I am saying is that whatever choice you make or are forced to make shouldn't be equated or compared and contrasted with the concept of having it all, because having it all is just a goddamn sham. And again, why is having it all so played up, as if by definition it is positive?

Is it the idea that women are afraid of missing out on anything, so we grab a little bit of "it all," and deem ourselves "well rounded"? To me that is much less "having it all" than "DOING it all." Big difference.

I have a few opinions on all of this. Number one: there is an ironic correlation between trying to "have it all," and winding up doing EVERYTHING, until you almost wind up in the hospital for exhaustion; number two: the propaganda of "you could have it all" has actually shifted to imply "you *should* have it all," which translates to "if you don't, you've done something wrong and totally suck"; number three: the propaganda has been spread with the sole purpose of splitting a powerful majority of the population and dividing it to conquer it; and number four, and the most important, so as the world becomes more and more obnoxiously expensive that you can't keep a roof over your head or go to a fucking baseball game for less than $500, women who have to work fifty-five-plus hours a week to make ends meet will be programmed to believe it's because they are "having it all," and not fucking slaving away to the masters of the universe!

If You Can't Have It All, What Can You Have?

Good question, and it's the question I think that should be asked and discussed because the answers that come from this will actually mean something for our self-esteem, productivity, relationships, satisfaction, and on and on. Instead of focusing on the differences between us à la the Mommy Wars, a.k.a., *she* doesn't work, and *I* do, or vice versa, how about focusing on what we all have in common as women: WE DON'T FUCKING HAVE IT ALL.

She runs her own company and needs to head overseas and will miss her son reading his first book by himself.

She is stuck at a PTA meeting with half a room of women with whom she would never actually choose to socialize, while her old colleagues are heading out for drinks at Rothmann's.

She put on fifteen pounds since she went back to work.

She got super skinny doing Pilates all week long, but has no life and no interests other than her kids.

She's a doctor who just turned forty-four and is freezing her one viable egg in the event her ex-boyfriend, whom she should've married fourteen years ago, leaves his wife and kids to come back and make a baby with her.

· *She* doesn't have kids, but has two million dollars in annuities. (Okay, this bitch actually wins.)

Everyone sacrifices in one form or another. Something always has to give. Maybe you're a business owner who thought you'd take your business to the "next level," and found you didn't have the time, energy, or inclination any longer. Or maybe you put all of yourself into growing the business, but that meant that your husband had to go to his own client dinners without you, when you would have liked to be there to support him. Maybe your art will always be there, but the tooth fairy days won't.

A good friend describes herself as feeling like she has a constant low-grade anxiety because she is still trying to have it all. She hasn't dropped the act. "It's that feeling of 'something' under your skin at all times." She is so insecure, though, and so in need of validation that I think she is just in love with being able to say she has it all rather than actually enjoying having it all. Don't we all have a little bit of that? By the way, having it all is not an ongoing state of being—the Having It All state, where you swarm around like a female version of Inspector Gadget, pulling shit and talents and ideas out from under your trench coat.

Drop the act: Working, not working, gestating, not gestating, planning to, not planning to, whatever, YOU CANNOT HAVE IT ALL. And just like the fish that doesn't soar over mountaintops, or the woman who doesn't scratch her balls, it was meant to be that way. One thing at a goddamn time!

If you're anything like me and decide you had it all, then you'll know how it feels: basically like being forced to work around six other people's schedules and ask permission for their help in order to make your life work.

Whatever you want to do with your time when you are not with your family—be it work a traditional job, write, make art, go to the gym, have an affair, whatever—the bottom line is you need to work your needs around the needs of everybody else and their mothers.

YOU: Hi, what are you doing next week? I might have to work, so I'll need you a few extra hours.

BABYSITTER: Oh, it's Valentine's Day, so Mike promised me he'd take me to this amazing restaurant that doesn't have a prix fixe menu.

HUSBAND: I have a late meeting and then the chiropractor that day.

MOTHER: Dad has his colonoscopy, and I promised your brother I'd watch his cat.

Ask the old lady up the block, who every Halloween offers to babysit: *Oh, honey, I've got that church thing. Bless your little heart.* Your cousin, but she has her women's group, and her daughter who has her culinary delights meeting, and her grandmother who has bridge, and finally the one person you could respect for telling you the goddamn truth, your father-in-law: "I just don't do kids." Bless *your* heart, Dad.

I toy with the idea of typing up these excuses and shoving them in little pink slips, so my clients could just hand them back to me with "You're fired." As if who the hell is going to take me seriously when I am the one left holding the bag of shit, which is in the form of my "having it all."

Then when I get stressed out, which is outwardly rare, I hear my mother and my husband in agreement over (finally) one thing: "Your health is more important. I don't know why you take on so much." Take on so much? Like more than who? I mean . . . *whom*? Brian? You? What am

I doing that you haven't been fucking priming me for my goddamn life. I have it all, don't you see?

And now that I have them both scared, I finish with this. And, if I don't do "too much," how will it get done? Who is going to do it? Yahoody, the man who turns your refrigerator light on?

You can't have it all. I don't care what it looks like. . . . I look for an interesting supporting part about once a year. That's the most I can manage. Some women can do it and that's fantastic, but I can't.

—Gwyneth Paltrow

I read a book called *The One Thing*. It is the most brilliant book because the author, Gary Keller, takes a concept so

---

There, I Said It! Ode to Boss

Dear Boss,

I'm sorry I can't work today. I dropped a bottle of nail polish on my cat and he has a shard of glass lodged in his eye, and needs a full-body shave, and after I drop my four-year-old off at pre-K, so he can become the next Mark Zuckerberg, I have to drop a bunch of paperwork off to my husband because he left it at home and since he has the job with the benefits (so I can be the amazing entrepreneur that I am), I am, well, sort of eating his shit on a daily basis and kinda have to help him out here, sooo . . . might not make this deadline. Thanks.

And if it's a guy, and he has a wife, don't expect sympathy. BUT, if he's a guy, who has a college-age daughter, YOU ARE GOLDEN because he is the man who thinks he is doing his talented, beautiful, apple-of-his-eye little girl a service by supporting her with, "Of course, you can have it all, sweetie."

---

obvious and older than time itself—tackle one thing at a time—and makes it sound like it's the first time anyone has ever thought of it. Anyway, it marries the myth of multitasking with making a one-item to-do list, and shows how productivity and success increase with the decrease in things to do.

Here's why you should drop the act: When you lean in to have it all, just remember that means you are going to have to lean out of something else.

You'll have more family time. Because doing whatever it is that you love, whether that's your business, your career, your hobby, you will be giving up family time. There is no other way to be a success outside of your home, if you don't put in your ten thousand hours doing that thing. And that is likely to mean you'll need to be away from the fam.

You'll have something for yourself. By giving up the idea or the pressure of having to have it all, maybe you'll actually drop the act and find something that you truly love for yourself. I had a friend who was just working like a maniac, having the kids, and everything in between, but was doing it because she thought it was a status sign of doing everything right in life—remember that state of being, that is not really a state of being? Anyway, turns out she didn't even like what she was doing anymore. Once she dropped the act, she freed up a whole shitload of her day to find out what did she want to have for herself. Funny how things work out like that.

If I always had to depend on my husband, I'd jump off a bridge. But it took me a long time to reconcile the fact that you don't have to be running American Express, either. I wake up, and I'm a real person. When did that happen? I am responsible for children, and I want to do the best I can do and instill the values in my children. I like for my daughters to see me working but not because I *have it all* and that I think women *should* work, but because I am choosing to spend some time in my day doing what makes me happy. That's what I want them to know—what makes them happy, and that they should just do it.

8

The Act: Better to Be Safe Than Sorry

Why to Drop the Act: Because a woman who dares greatly takes one giant leap for womankind

You can't stay relevant unless you're pushing yourself out onto the razor's edge of life on a regular basis.

—Madonna

*I*magine at the age of eleven or twelve, writing a blog under a pseudonym that shares the horrors of your life living under the occupation of the Taliban, and advocating the right of education for girls who were prevented from going to school under Taliban rule. Then after garnering attention for your precocious endeavors, you're nominated for the International Children's Peace Prize by South African activist Desmond Tutu. Then imagine boarding your school bus, having a gunman call you by name, point a pistol at you, and fire three shots. You pull yourself out of critical condition, only to find that there is a fatwa called in your honor, and the Taliban retaliates with promises to kill you next time. Instead of going into hiding, you speak out and become known as a Pakistani activist for female education and the youngest-ever Nobel Prize laureate. This is the story of Malala Yousafzai.

Can you even fathom having one ounce of the determination that Hyvon Ngetich had, when she led the elite women's division of the Austin Marathon with three miles remaining, only to have her body give out? As she dropped to the ground, the finish line was only a few hundred yards away. When race volunteers came up from behind her with a wheelchair to take her to the finish line, she didn't want a part of it. Getting such help would've disqualified her. So what did the twenty-nine-year-old from Kenya do? She crawled.

What about swimming across the Atlantic Ocean? Have that one on your to-do list? Yeah, me too. Can you even wrap your head around the story of the fifty-six-year-old Jennifer Figge, who left the Cape Verde Islands off Africa's western coast on January 12, 2009, but not in a plane—in the water! She fought waves of up to thirty feet along with strong winds and kept in touch with her friend via satellite phone. She reached Trinidad less than a month later and became the first woman on record to swim across the Atlantic Ocean.

I know what you're thinking because I was thinking it, too: I should just give it up now! While I certainly feel like I swim across an ocean on a daily basis, the only place I ever crawl to is into my bed!

I've always taken risks, and never worried what the world might really think of me.

—Cher

These stories and many others of extreme dares keep my eyes glued to the television or rewinding YouTube over and over until I've shed enough tears to fill an ocean, but, still, I don't want to *be* these women. Not because I wouldn't want to carb up for months on end or make the cover of the *New York Times*, but because I know it's a waste of time to compare myself to anybody else but me. What these stories do for me, however, and hopefully for you, is make me want to be a better me; to figure out ways that I can dare greatly in my mundane life.

Brené Brown wrote a book called *Daring Greatly* that I think everyone should read, and if you don't have the time, definitely check out Brené's TED talks. Wow! What Brené wants us to know about daring greatly is not that we should tightrope walk across the Golden Gate Bridge or plan Houdini stunts on a daily basis or even swim across the Atlantic. In fact, that's not her idea of daring at all. Daring greatly, according to her research, means being vulnerable and putting ourselves out there in ways that make us feel exposed. Because she has found that it is in these moments—the ones where we are forced outside our comfort zones—that we have the potential to grow and develop. When I think about it, the topics discussed throughout this book (okay, maybe not discussed, more ranted) really boil down to fear of vulnerability. That's why we adopt these acts in the first place, isn't it? Having a hard time pumping enough milk for your newborn? You don't dare broadcast that; you adopt an act. Secretly having a hard time staying on your diet? You don't dare admit to everyone at your WW meeting that you eat peanut butter out of the jar with a fork at 2 a.m. because you find it comforting. (Oh, is that TMI, as if I care?) Haven't had sex with your spouse in two months? Don't dare to share that with a girlfriend or else she might judge your marriage.

So we huff and we puff and we blow more hot air, and that is not daring greatly at all. Brené Brown explains that when we pretend in life, when we wear masks and adopt acts, it is because we are attempting to protect our lives against bad things. As she says, "How can anything go wrong when my life looks like an ad?"

Dropping the act and saying we are not the Happy Homemaker icon in a 1960s vacuum cleaner ad is literally the ultimate Daring Greatly moment—a moment where you just turn to another person—friend or foe, stranger or relative—and say, Take me or leave me, or as I would say, "If you don't like it, tough shit."

"That's right, I just fed my kid Similac, bitch."

I like to think that when I wrote this book, I dared greatly, but I did so only with the sincere hope that you will dare greatly, too, and embrace all your craziness and weakness and awesome gifts and talents, and put yourself out there.

So don't think that you have to do some crazy ass shit like tightrope walk across the Golden Gate Bridge or eat slug pie on some stupid reality show, or worst of all, rub your husband's feet! Daring greatly can be exhibited by the mom who speaks up at the Board of Ed meeting because her son's services were cut. It's the woman who says "I'm sorry" to her best friend for saying out-of-order things when she was drunk. It's the woman who tells her husband she is having dreams about a man at work because she's feeling ignored. It's the woman who runs the first 5K of her life at the age of seventy-five. It's the woman who sends back her food because it's not cooked the way she wants and doesn't apologize for it! We dare greatly when we decide to get pregnant, quit our jobs, start a business, admit our weaknesses, or yell at a friend's boyfriend for being a douchebag.

This is what daring greatly looks like in real life, in your life, and it's "little" things like this that are capable of spreading goodwill, increasing self-esteem, setting standards for our children, and effecting change on a grassroots level. Okay, I'll get off my soapbox now. So where do you begin if you're not like me—a giant big mouth? Well, I say daring greatly begins with daring to speak up, have a voice, and be unapologetic for your point of view.

When I dare to be powerful—to use my strength in the service of my vision, then it becomes less and less important whether I am afraid.

—Audre Lorde

Speak Up

Sheryl Sandberg said it much more eloquently when she wrote her book *Lean In*. What a hem-haw that was. But once you clear away the noise surrounding women and careers, take away the politics and the economics, and silence the "debates" and op-ed pieces, all the Facebook exec is saying to women is "Speak up!"

So, what's the problem?

The problem is that for many women, even today, speaking up is one of the hardest things to do, and who can blame us? With people so quick to judge, technology's ability to irreversibly transmit our opinions and outbursts over the Internet, only to be frozen there for eternity, and women's natural fear of not being liked, it's no wonder why "speak up and be seen" seems just too much a hassle.

Working as one of the editors in the early years at *Oprah* magazine, I was exposed to the culture of "speak up and be seen" on a daily basis. It goes without saying that Oprah was the first woman to empower an insanely large amount of women in just fifty minutes' time to just say "it"—whether that "it" was a secret binging habit, an irrational fear of plastic, or the inability to have children. When Oprah spoke up about taboo subjects, private issues, or personal history, she did so to her audience's benefit because we all learned something through her outspokenness. Oprah shocked the world by not only talking about her fat, but wheeling in its weight equivalent in lard on Radio Flyer wagons (I stress multiple wagons) for the world to see. Talk about a visual. And speaking of visuals, remember when she planted Dr. Oz on the map by talking about poo—specifically women's poo (as if we poo!). That discussion changed the way women viewed and assessed their health—forever.

Hell, the combination of Oprah's ability to call out the elephant in the room was legitimized because she didn't do it for entertainment's sake; she did it because it came from a real place of wanting to inform and empower. When I was working at the magazine, I might have taken my lessons of speak up a bit too literally, but looking back, I'm glad I said what I said, even though I almost ruined a perfectly nice Passover meal at my childhood friend's home.

There's something liberating about not pretending. Dare to embarrass yourself. Risk.

—Drew Barrymore

There we all were, old family friends from the neighborhood, Jill and her boyfriend, Brian and me, sitting at the Passover dinner table, "enjoying" gefilte fish and horseradish . . . speed-eating matzo on our way to dessert. Now if any of you celebrate Passover, you know that Pesach desserts are pretty much disgusting (that is, if you really "keep" Pesach)! Leslie (the boyfriend . . . in case the name confused you) brought a chocolate cake, and everyone was really ready to dig in! As Jill's mother was passing pieces out to everyone, Leslie turned to Jill and said, "I'm not sure you should be taking such a large piece of cake."

HALT.

I don't think everyone at the table heard this, but I was certain my ears were not deceiving me. I must have really wanted that cake because I let the first comment slide and stuffed a few loaded forkfuls down myself. As Jill reached out to accept her mother's second sliver, Leslie said, with disgust in his voice, "Jill, I think one piece is enough for you; do you really need a second piece?"

DING DING DING DING. It was as if Pavlov's bell was ringing (except these bells in my head sounded more like the Round 1 bell at an Ultimate Fighting match) because my response was salivation—I wanted blood.

"Um, excuse me." I really had no intention of being excused, and continued my interrogation. "Are you suggesting that she not have another piece, and if so, for what reason?" Somehow, Leslie sensed that it was a rhetorical question, because he didn't answer the question. "Do you honestly think it's appropriate to monitor what a thirty-year-old woman chooses to eat?"

One who, BTW, is fit, healthy, and eats well? *Not* that it would make a difference either way, but it did just make it *that* much more infuriating!

My husband gave me that look and then bowed his head in his typical style that resembles a man in prayer mode, desperately bargaining with God (or whomever) to make whatever I was about to do get over with pronto and with relatively minor amounts of casualty and scar tissue. Looking around the silent room, it was like one of those images from Leonardo da Vinci's *The Last Supper* because the entire family was in some sort of prayer mode position. It was a holiday, after all, albeit the wrong one.

"Leslie," I continued, and then in one breath spewed, "*I* think you need to sit there and not say anything more, for fear I will continue to *monitor* everything you say—and eat—which can and will get ugly."

I, and pretty much everyone who loves me, am aware of my irritable vowel syndrome, where I get the verbal runs, but this outburst was definitely one for the books. I have to say, I don't have regrets, and in the end, silence wasn't golden. "C'mon," I begged, "by saying nothing, we're condoning this crap." The collective groan was acknowledgment enough for me.

As much as the next person, I've heard of the psychological term "projection" and will admit that my own struggles with food and body image at various points in my life probably contributed to my having to see a little justice for Jill and for all.

The morals of the story: (1) Eat cake if you want to. (2) Have a second helping if you want to. If you date a guy named Leslie, who has a problem with numbers one and two, then here's moral number three: dump the douchebag.*

Aside from having to put occasional machismo into its place, I think that women need to speak up because when they do, they share information and learn things. Speak up and watch each other grow smarter and more prepared. I want women to be outspoken and informed; in fact, could you imagine a more beautiful combination?

Most people live and die with their music still unplayed. They never dare to try.

—Mary Kay Ash

Being Outspoken about Being Outspoken

I'm outspoken to say the least, and while I realize that attribute (yes, it's an attribute!) alone doesn't make me very interesting, or "credentialed" enough to discuss this topic, the idea that so many women are *not* saying what's on their minds is what I believe to be the root of an insidious identity crisis. We're hiding ourselves. Statistics show that women's Achilles heel is still politeness, whether when negotiating salaries, asking spouses to help fold the damn fitted sheets, or taking on too many duties. For women, outspoken should no longer be synonymous with meanness, giving unsolicited advice or unconstructive criticism. Speaking up is not being disrespectful or unsupportive. So, then what the hell is it?

Outspoken (adj.): 1. uttered or expressed with frankness or without reserve: outspoken criticism; 2. free or unreserved in speech

---

* Jill passed over Leslie and is now married to someone else. Mazel!

Free. Free to be ourselves!

So if one is not outspoken, what is she? I took to the antonyms section of Dictionary.com and zeroed in on the word "taciturn."

Taciturn (adj.): reluctant to share/join in the conversation

OMG, that's so sad. Are such women therefore so trapped in their own politeness or passivity that they miss out on *the conversation? Our* conversation? The one that women should be having with one another so as to support, encourage, and cheer on one another, instead of being catty or divisive on sideshow debates that don't matter in the long run? This leads back to Sheryl Sandberg, who got sandblasted by her own kind—women—for what? For simply saying, "Join in the conversation; don't be taciturn!"

If you dare greatly by speaking up and dropping the act of pretending to be polite when your friend is being abused by an asshole like Leslie, then you contribute to the conversation. About women, what we go through, what we fear, what we shouldn't be afraid of. It's sharing information about our vulnerabilities, mistakes, regrets, humiliations in the name of freeing us from the silence of our own shame. Is that hyperbolic? Sure, why not! I've been known to be that, too.

Go with Your Gut

Sometimes daring greatly just means going with your gut, especially when it seems that the logical answer has already presented itself. Are you the type that plans out

---

There, I Said It!

I see myself in my girls, and I know when you are at that impressionable age (my girls are eight and four), daring greatly is almost impossible, especially if you a girl. Speaking your mind to friends at that age can be dicey at best, and you are never sure how they will react. You constantly hear things like "I don't want to be your friend" or "You hurt my feelings." Friends don't always get your humor, and they almost always don't understand sensitivity. It's a hard combination at such a young age to know pretty much exactly what you like and what you don't like, but the world is still catching up to your candor, and that's the critical point where girls, if misguided, may choose to adjust the gift of candor and kowtow to the world (a.k.a. adopt the act).

I am finally at a point in my life where I truly don't care who can handle me and who cannot. If you don't like the smell, get out of the kitchen. By the way, daring greatly is not to be confused with not giving a shit; it's the contrary. It's the ability to express how you feel, in the way you feel most natural, while honoring your true self in the process. You would be surprised how real your relationships—even the most casual ones—can become when you let it all hang out. I'm still learning every day to adapt to a world that does not necessarily work the way I do and to find those unique and special individuals who share similar views. Being yourself is sometimes the biggest dare you can ever take.

---

the giant leap off of a high dive, after contemplating just about everything before you do . . . weighing the good and the bad about your decision and coming to a complete standstill? Or are you like me and you just rip the fucking Band-Aid off as fast and as hard as you possibly can? Someone once said to me, "The most constant thing in life is change," so I would rather be the person who embraces it than shies away from it. I mean, shit, if it's going to happen anyway, I might as well have a handle on it.

Now, this is not to say I don't have a deep respect for women who are analytical, but I do think there is a tendency to overthink things. And when biology has given women the awesome gift of intuition, why neglect it? Of course, there is a fine line between being a risk taker and just being stupid. . . . I have certainly been both. But I have found that the risks, as hard as they were on me and in some cases on people I loved, never hurt me. In the past five to seven years, I have taken an incredible amount of risks, from moving out of my comfort zone (NYC) to the suburbs to launching my own business and closing it to launching another business and writing a book. I'm not saying this to seem like I live propped up on my high horse; I say it because of the tremendous pain I know comes along with daring greatly. This book might flop or get ripped by reviewers. Maybe you'll even write me for your money back (I dared greatly just now by even planting *that* seed!), but I just know that this process has already paid me back in dividends in the form of life lessons, which will almost 100 percent come in handy in some way at some other time in a totally unrelated experience. I just know it, because that's what my gut tells me. Listening to the wisdom of my instinct that says, "This isn't about reviews, it's not about sales," feels like daring greatly to me. But really, what would I gain if I ignored my intuition and allowed my right brain to tell my left brain lies about how this book will land me my own talk show and how safe it is out there in the wonderful world of publishing? The fact of the matter is, I will fail more than I will succeed, as long as I dare greatly. Unfortunately we have a propensity to remember only the failures and the bad stuff rather than the good times. And when that happens, listen to your gut and let it tell you what you know is true: I'd rather have dared than not have done anything at all.

When I left magazines and dove into a part of the industry I had no experience in (public relations), I jumped in with both feet. It was an executive position, and I had little to no idea what I was doing; I dared greatly and prayed nightly! But my gut told me that I was made to be a publicist, although I could never have been so successful in that area without my past experience in magazines. Each "daring greatly" move propelled me further into my career and allowed me to be a better media person due to each experience before that.

When I opened my own business, I had no idea the magnitude of what I was doing and what it would lead me to do. How many amazing clients I would meet and how many brands I would touch. How I would somehow walk away with a book deal, the concept for a new company, and so many amazing experiences with my business partner.

And then there's the book. After so many years of people telling me to be less honest and less forthright, to not "overshare" (whatever the hell that means), all the times teachers said to me that you can't write like you talk, well here I am. I am a big believer that if I didn't believe there was a need for this then I wouldn't write it. If I didn't "dare greatly" by listening to my gut, then it would never have happened. (My brain was fighting my gut the whole way!)

I realized that the majority of people do respond positively to candor, that they do appreciate when the veil is lifted, when the act is dropped and the real self is revealed to others. I find strength in vulnerability and not shame.

Opening your mouth when no one else will, making sure your point gets across no matter how uncomfortable the conversation becomes, that's daring greatly. Letting everyone know that you shit DOES in fact stink, dropping the holier-than-thou act, that's daring greatly. Defending people is my biggest daring greatly move yet, and the one that I am most proud of. When I see someone prey on others, my animal instincts kick in and I am like a lion on the prowl. If you can't do it for yourself I am right there for you, and there is very little that can stop me. But ultimately what I intend to happen is not for that person to always come running to me as if I were her bodyguard, but to see that nothing but good happens when you speak up, and then decide to do it for herself.

Stop Hoping

One last way that I try to dare greatly is by letting go of hope. What, you say? Why would anyone think it is brave to stop hoping? Because that's who I am. I'm more of a "tangible, show me the empirical evidence" kind of gal, than an "if I will it, it will come" person. I'm not judging anyone who sends positive messages to the universe and hopes for the universe to respond. Absolutely, more power to you. But I am, by nature, a doer, so it seems too much a time suck to be on the universe's time, when I might be able to do something myself to speed up the process of getting whatever it is I'm after.

We have to dare to be ourselves, however frightening or strange that self may prove to be.

—May Sarton

How is it a daring greatly moment to stop hoping? Because when you stop hoping for something, you are actually choosing to believe in yourself and in your own power to make things happen. Wow, to believe in yourself—no doubts, no act necessary, just you and your goal? Is there anything more daring than that?

It's go time!

9

The Act: Look How Far We've Come

Why to Drop the Act: Because progress can't happen if we keep lying to ourselves and everyone else

Civilized society is perpetually menaced with disintegration through this primary hostility of men towards one another.

—Sigmund Freud

We've come a long way, baby! When it comes to American idioms, this is probably one of the most versatile. It's been a theme in politics, in various movements—like civil rights and women's liberation—in country songs, in wartime and peacetime, in careers and family, in romance and breakups, and, of course, most famously, as the vintage slogan for Virginia Slims cigarettes. While I would love to go with the flow and admit that, yes, when it comes to smoking (cigarettes), we've come a long way baby toward quitting, my ideological side takes a backseat to the logical side, the side that actually sees, takes note, and processes what is truly going on: progress is an illusion—*an act* we hide behind. We hope to pretend our flawed traits of bigotry, jealousy, insecurity, greed, gluttony, ignorance, whatever, have evolved into civilized traits like cooperation, equality, strength, empathy, compassion, support, charity, and education, but, in most cases, it's just bullshit. Drop the act. At its core, society is acting no better than it did sixty years ago.

Sure, we might not have magazine advertisements, like the one for Mr. Leggs that shows a man standing on an animal skin rug, foot atop the head of a woman, headline reading, "It's nice to have a woman around the house." Long way we've come in advertising, but the truth is, women are still fighting for equal pay and are still running around half-naked twerking in order to get men's attention, and lamenting to each other over coffee about unequal distribution of household duties!

Or what about the ad for Camels that stated, "More doctors smoke Camels than any other cigarette!" Long way? Yes, I suppose, the number of teens smoking cigarettes is now low, but I'm still deciding how the hell we've managed to increase heroin overdoses by 39 percent in ONE YEAR, according to the Centers for Disease Control. Haven't we been fighting some war on drugs since the eighties? When I hear from friends of teenagers that high school raves of the eighties and nineties have been replaced by RX swaps in the basement of rich people's houses, it seems to me the "war on drugs" has become another Vietnam.

It goes without saying, even though I do like to be redundant at times for emphasis' sake, that it is my belief that we haven't come very far at all. Just because the target may be different doesn't mean the behavior has changed. Pretty cynical, I know. But my unique perspective of having a toe dipped in many different worlds—black, white, Jewish, atheist, rich, poor, married, divorced, educated, uneducated, working mom, stay-at-home mom, city, suburb—I've experienced these lifestyles that have supposedly come a long way and stand mystified by the still very poor behavior on the parts of all types against all other types.

In short, we are still very much uncivilized! And you know why? Because people are fucking narcissists. They think this is their world, and we're just living in it. This becomes scarily real to me as I defensively drive on the New Jersey Turnpike, cut off by guys with small dicks driving big cars and no indicator blinking. At least once a day I yell, "What am I, invisible?" as another asshole on his headset almost clips me.

Then the women who ruin my one attempt a month to actually take thirty minutes of "me" time and have my nails done by sitting in their pedicure chairs talking loudly on their cell phones, as if we were all in their living rooms. SHUT UP! Short of a medical emergency with your kid or a life-threatening situation, and maybe a work crisis, IT CAN WAIT! What I have to withstand is the yapping about Amy's kid's Bar Mitzvah, sweet sixteen, or whatever event of the century happening this Saturday, and what nail color would go with the perfect pair of Jimmy Choos. Or the mom talking to the other mom about the house they are selling and how they need to spruce it up to show it for the open house over the weekend. I mean, naturally, these poor women are burdened with life-and-death situations.

And the business owner, who actually expects patrons to give him repeat business, who spews off-color comments about different socioeconomic populations, many of whom he "services."

The lovely construction worker who hollers at me on a Manhattan side street, while I'm eight months' pregnant no less. Even I don't want to fuck me, so how he does is beyond me. My favorite indication, though, that we are a community of savages, is how we act as such in front of our own offspring, ensuring the fact that we can look forward to yet another generation of assholes that will never help society progress. I mean, moms, do you really feel justified cutting the car line at school pickup? Watch out! I am coming for you.

And then the woman who is not at all a racist, in fact, she prides herself on the fact that she has so many friends who are black and Latino, and tells everyone so, not realizing how fucking racist that comment is. My personal all-time favorite, the women (not typically men) who in my local Starbucks ask me if I need additional work in the home, and do I have a cell number that they can use to reach me to help take care of their child. I am not a fucking nanny! Although, there's nothing wrong with being one at all, but I wonder why, given we have come such a "long way," you assume a woman with darker skin holding the hand of a head-to-toe adorable blonde child must be the help. These same women, by the way, are the ones who go up to white women at gymnastics and congratulate them on the adoption of their beautiful child from China, only for the half-Asian husband to walk into the room.

Gee, I don't know about you, but this all happened in my world, oh, around last week. Long way? Yeah . . . no.

Don't get me wrong. It's nice to want to change and try to change, but frankly, I'm feeling a bit hopeless in our ability to make it stick. I mean, how is it that we live in a world where we can reach for any device and "Face-Time" those we love, study Mars from the comforts of

Earth, and save a life on the brink of death on the daily, but can't seem to all get along, or at the very least accept each other? I sound so cliché and so incredibly naïve to think that I once thought that by the time I had kids the world would've been a different place; that views would somehow change and that people would love everyone for who they are, not what they are. . . . Kum-ba-fucking-yah. Damn was I wrong, and not like a little bit wrong, like horrifically wrong.

The Amazing Race

There were always so many raw emotions growing up when it came to discussions about my mom's family, and where they were my entire childhood. When my white debutante midwestern mother chose to marry "someone like my father," i.e., black, from upper Manhattan, self-made, she did so at the risk of losing her entire family, from which she was ultimately cast out. It's amazing to me to think that a difference of color or religion could be something that could potentially break a family apart. That people would be willing to lose their relationship with their own child, and then the offspring of that child, or any family member for that matter, simply because she did not end up with someone exactly like them. The adversities she was up against were ones that no one should have to endure, but nonetheless, I see it now going on forty years later as I am now part of an "interracial, interreligious" marriage and family of my very own. Stares, double takes, mistaken for a nanny, the progress is nowhere to be seen.

My husband, Brian, followed in my mother's foot-steps when he fell in love with me and geared up for the inevitable conversation about my ethnic and religious background, mostly the latter. He wasn't risking being shunned or anything as ludicrous as that, but let's face it, JDate and Christian Mingle weren't invented because people are comfortable mixing religions. So, my not being Jewish was going to be a family "discussion," to say the least. Good news is that it was a fleeting moment, and we have since never looked back, but at the time, did it infuriate me? *Yes!* Did I understand or could I relate to those feelings? *No!* Did we move forward and do we have a loving relationship with his family? *Yes!* People can change; they need to be shown the way.

> *No one is born hating another person because of the color of his skin, or his background or his religion. People learn to hate, and if they can learn to hate, they can be taught love, for love comes more naturally to the human heart than its opposite.*

—Nelson Mandela

Unfortunately, it doesn't seem like there's enough people working to spread the good, so we keep losing out to the mass of bad. If I have learned one thing growing up in a mixed household it was to judge people "not by the color of their skin, but on the content of their character" (Dr. Martin Luther King Jr.). Problem is too many people weren't taught those sentiments! I would like to think we have come to a time where my generation feels differently than the generation preceding us, so as to not teach our children the hate that they themselves were taught; but clearly that's not the case for everyone. The issue is those "other people" are still living that same bigoted life. They are shopping in our supermarkets, teaching in our schools,

There, I Said It! Get a Real Cause for Complaint

When I walk into a room with my United Nations family, I feel so incredibly lucky to look like we do. A melting pot of love brought together to make one big piece of Americana that includes a little bit of everything. We are happy (most of the time) and celebrate all of our differences, whether it be skin and hair color or religion. We get to celebrate a million beautiful holidays and traditions with both sides of our family, while teaching our girls to love all the beautiful differences that make us a unique and special family.

I am still perplexed by people who send holiday cards that read Happy Hanukkah or Merry Christmas, as opposed to what I think should be the norm for everyone, Happy Holidays. And then, I am further perplexed by the audacity people have when they publicly talk about how "insulted" or bothered they are when they receive a card that doesn't specifically reference their particular holiday. Who the fuck cares? You should be happy I thought enough to waste a freaking stamp on you. Please, find a real cause!

How is it that we still live in a world where we only surround ourselves with people who are exactly like us? Don't we want to see the world in all its many colors and all its glory? Don't people want to get to know people who are not exactly like them? I am not going so far as to say you can't be with someone who is in many ways like you, but if that's the motivation, don't you risk being with people for all of the wrong reasons? Or are you with them because everything seems like it would be easier if you were with someone who looked like you in the mirror? Or if that's what you choose, are you still able to appreciate all of the differences the world has to offer? And can you do so in a way that does not make people who are in mixed relationships or have mixed kids feel so ostracized in society? How's that for a four-course meal of food for thought!

owning our hair salons—spewing the uneducated hatred when and wherever they can, to whomever they can.

Mad Money? Or Money Gone Mad?

Here's a nice little irony for you. Today, more people take up yoga, read books on Buddhism, and claim to "meditate" than ever before, yet we are more materialistic than ever! When it comes to getting our priorities right in this world, I don't see how we've come a long way. I'm not even going to reference the fact that douchebag Wall Street do-nothings command a higher paycheck than people who actually make a difference in this world (oops, just did). What I see is this pervasive competition to one-up each other materialistically. Don't know about you, but that doesn't seem like progress to me.

I remember a time in my life when I went sweet sixteen hopping, then graduation party hopping, then wedding hopping. It all boiled down to whose party was more lavish, who had a better pop star come and "surprise" them for a performance at their party, or whose dress was a true one-of-a-kind Vera Wang (me included). But the real trouble started when these people started procreating. Then the real competition started. Stop the ride, I want to get off.

I am not sure why each person/party felt like he had to outdo the next (serious penis envy), but it was a clear indication that the more you spent, the more money you wanted to show people you had. Now at the ripe old age of thirty-nine, I still can't shake the feeling that I am in a perpetual sweet sixteen party, surrounded by the same bullshit (with really great music!) except I am far more jaded!

I feel as if we are all living in our own little *Truman Show*, except we welcome it. We want to be seen, to be revered, idolized; and the downfall and dumbing down of media and social networking is certainly a big reason for that. We all really do believe we should put on a persona or adopt one for the world to see. And aside from how beautiful or successful we are or aren't, at the core of it is financial wealth, and the evidence of it.

Why is it that grown-ass women don't have the ability to realize that putting an emphasis on what their husbands (or they) do for a living and how much they make does not validate who they are . . . or does it? Clotaire Rapaille, a French-born American market researcher, explored this question in his book *The Culture Code*. In one of his chapters of his book, titled "Working for a Living: The Codes for Work and Money," Rapaille posits that our need to show how much we achieve through work is basically an American phenomenon.

"The American Culture Code for Work is WHO YOU ARE. . . . When we ask someone what she does for a living, we ask her who she is."

I think this is where what I call Rich Bitch Syndrome comes from. Clearly someone who can't sit at dinner with the girls without slipping in something about her eighty-dollar eyelash extensions, $35,000 Hermes bag, or obscene tuition payment her accountant just made to Darian's private nursery school doesn't know who she is, so she hides behind the act of being a woman of substance, literally and figuratively.

Rapaille further states, "Americans rarely accept a dead end in their jobs without a fight, and they strongly believe that you are only as good as your last deal. A billionaire still works sixty hours a week because he needs constant affirmation of who he is."

We need to affirm ourselves in this way? This is the best way we can figure out how to justify our existence?! It seems yes. We are the same old person we were when we were twelve, sixteen, twenty for Christ's sake! Insecure with little self-esteem and a lot to feel threatened by. Even as adults we act like jealous, narcissistic, one-upper kids. Me included! And just like it was not a cute look at twenty, it's not a cute look at forty. I have fallen victim to this negative and small behavior, trapped in a conversation, feeling like my back is against a wall, my animal instincts coming out for the defensive kill. The difference is now that I have dropped the act, owning the fact that when I act this small I prove I haven't "come very far," I check myself right back into my reality and remind myself that I have already determined what really is important to me in this world, and it's not whatever this chick is talking about. The problem is, we need more people to check themselves, or else the game will continue, and our self-worth will never be tied to our "content," but to our context.

Showing off is a fool's idea of glory.

—Bruce Lee

I'm *So* Not That Person Anymore

With each phase of life, people believe they evolve and change in some fundamental way. While I certainly do hope that is the case, when the going gets tough and we find ourselves under pressure, some things never change.

There, I Said It! "I Live in a Million-Dollar House with My Eight-Million-Dollar Mouth!"

Gone are the days when you don't talk about money; here are the days when you literally count your "dollar, dollar bills y'all." Gone are the days when living on the east vs. west side of town simply meant geography; here are the days when you feel like you hit your quota if you have a friend from the other side of town. Why are we so afraid and insecure that we won't be liked unless we precede our reputation with what our financial status is? I welcome making millions and everything that goes along with it, I mean, shit, who doesn't, but I don't welcome it with your eight-million-dollar mouth. If you can please refrain from letting everyone in the free world know how much you are made of, because it just sends a message of what you are not.

It's the closest thing we come to time travel, in my opinion—the phenomenon of being transported back into our bodies and minds of our weakest, most vulnerable (most of the time younger) selves.

Ninety percent of the time I know exactly who I am. I recognize myself, my responses, my thoughts, my feelings. Then when something happens, something I can't quite control, I feel like I'm in *Back to the Future*. The moment I can't quite catch my breath because the flood of familiar feelings comes back, and I am that sixteen-year-old girl in her room, alone, looking out the window, with too much to think about.

There I was walking into a movie theater with my girls, semi-excited to see a G-rated movie, when I ran into HER. HER, who shall remain nameless, because I can't even say her name or else risk that I will Beetlejuice her and run into her again in the near future; three times to be exact. You know, the one you just wish left your brain when you left the friendship, or when the friendship ended. The one you would like to think evolved the way you think you have but alas not only looks the same, but acts the same . . . just worse. The HER to whom you screamed, "Karma's a bitch," yet she doesn't seem to be knee deep in anything remotely smelling like shit? The HER who if you mention the pronoun to any of your friends, they automatically know who you are talking about. Yes, HER. I stare as she continues to talk like she's getting paid to do so, and I just freeze—a deer in headlights. I don't talk back, even though my youngest daughter is poking me to make sure I haven't turned into petrified wood. What pains me most is that I've fantasized about this day, imagined running into HER, and me thrusting my fist toward her smug face and nailing her square between the eyes. I take a deep breath and exchange niceties, and reinforce to myself that not even in death will I ever be friends with HER again.

But instead of reveling in how far I've come, how happy I am, and how I managed to make a great life without her in it, I reverted back to this shaky, weak, vulnerable person, as if the hurt had just happened for the first time. Gee, I thought I was over it, but apparently my blood pressure isn't. I play the scene from ancient history over in my head as the words continue to fly out of her mouth like an adult on Charlie Brown—wah wah wah wah. What could I have done differently back then? How is she feeling about this run-in, and what happens the next time I fucking see her? Now seated, I move on to the next emotion while sitting and wallowing in an obsessive manner, that basically takes over "normal," sane thinking. I'm "watching" the movie now the same way you get somewhere when you autodrive a car and don't remember the driving-there part.

I don't feel that bad about accepting the fact that I am still the same person I have always been because I know of a neurosurgeon who experienced the same thing. He literally walked into his twenty-year high school reunion focused on his plan to really "show them all" how far he had come. He was known in his circle of medical geniuses as charismatic, and by all of the geniuses' wives as smoking hot. He was that kid in middle school you see now who you want to take aside and assure that one day he'll work his eyeglasses right into the hearts and imaginations of every woman he meets. Anyway, he no sooner walked through the doors of his damn high school gymnasium than he was transported back to his annoying shy self. His old squeaky nervous laugh emerged, one his wife had never even heard, his hands clammed up, and he became intent on finding a corner and staking his claim on it. *This was not a good idea,* he thought. His wife was stunned. As each old schoolmate came up to him and read his Hello My Name Is sticky name tag, this published MD couldn't look anyone square in the face.

How far do we ever really come? Reverting to old behaviors or to what we have learned (even if we know we're wrong) in our formative years is such a force that it actually explains a lot of the reason people in society don't seem to be getting as far ahead as we hope to or claim to.

Going the distance takes a lot of energy, focus, hard work, and admitting we are wrong—wrong in the way we treat one another, wrong in believing we are better or worse than anyone else, wrong in where our priorities lie, and especially wrong about our measure of progress. Only by dropping this act can we really establish how scared and isolated we feel. Only then will we gain the self-actualization required to change the world—for real.

> *You can close your eyes to the things you don't want to see, but you can't close your heart to the things you don't want to feel.*

—Johnny Depp

My wish for all of us is to find the courage to drop the act and become self-actualized, a concept defined as expressing one's creativity, quest for spiritual enlightenment, pursuit of knowledge, and desire to give to society. Abraham Maslow believed that only after the basic human needs—food, shelter, warmth, security, sense of belongingness, etc.—are met can self-actualization occur. It's the human need to be good, to be fully alive, and to find meaning in life.

Drop the act, so we can admit we need to first achieve those basics, and then do so, and finally make enough progress to move on to the part where we can all start living with meaning.

ACKNOWLEDGMENTS

*T*hank you to my daughters, Aiden Rae and Lila James, for inspiring me to be exactly who I want to be, and allowing their silly, crazy mom to enjoy every moment of being a parent. My own mother, Mama Elizabeth, I love you so much and could never repay you for devoting your entire life to your kids, sacrificing your own time (and sanity) simply raising us so well, solo. And to my father (God rest his soul) for being such a pain in my ass . . . it helped me channel *all* of my energy into dropping the act and speaking my mind.

Thank you to my brother Chip who knows me well enough to know that the fuck-you fist pump from *Friends* really means I love you the most!

To my big sisters Kim and Kelly even though we did not grow up together the traditional way, I feel so incredibly blessed to have you in my life every day.

To my girlfriends who let me be me without trying to change one little thing about me, even when you wanted to, my sincere love. And, of course, to all my guy friends who give me shit on the daily, but always with a huge smile and, more importantly, a drink in hand.

Thank you to my family for taking the time to watch the girls when I needed to work on the book. And to my friends' children for keeping Aiden and Lila occupied when I just didn't have it in me. There are so many people who sent countless, inspirational e-mails and with whom I had many a conversation about their enthusiasm for the book, and I thank you all for believing in me just because you love me.

I must acknowledge all of the people who helped inspire this book by being incredibly closed minded, limited, and ignorant. You have imbedded profound memories in my brain forever, and without you, there would be no act to drop.

I want to extend an enormous thanks to my writer Michele who listened to hours upon hours upon hours of my life and for helping to create a book that I am so, so, so proud of. I appreciate you more than you know.

Thank you to my former teacher, who told me that I could never be a successful writer, simply because I was not supposed to "write like you talk." Thank you to my sleepaway camp counselors and friends, who offered me an awesome respite, where I learned to speak up and be the truest version of myself, and which gave me my best friends (the three amigos) as a gift for life.

Thank you to my new New Jersey friends who showed me that there is life after New York City and that it is possible to create meaningful relationships with amazing, smart, kind, and progressive women later in life.

Thank you to Marta Hallett, who (by chance) read my journal, and not only encouraged me to write a book but pushed me forward so that I could do it. Thank you to my former agent who said this was not going to work out, which led me to my current agent Regina Brooks, who saw something in me that others didn't. Thank you to my teachers and countless other superiors who didn't deter me from speaking my mind but helped me channel it into something more impactful. Thank you to those who didn't believe in me; it just propelled me further into my career. Thank you to those who forgave me when I had a moment of weakness and was not the person I wanted to be; and a sincere apology if I ever made you feel anything less than stellar.

Thank you to all the women who speak their minds and are not afraid to change the world.

Thank you to my publisher for seeing the need for this book.

And finally, thank you to my partner in crime for the last twenty years, my husband, Brian, who has never tried to change me, alter me, or silence me. Thank you for allowing me to put it all out there and for doing everything you could to keep me sane. Thank you for allowing me to take risks even when the odds were stacked against me, and thank you for seeing the real me even when it is not so pretty.